Dads Like Us

*Raising a Child
with Disabilities*

Steve Harris

River
Place
Press

What Others Are Saying About "Dads Like Us"...

"This book hits the mark on what fathers need to know to support the needs of their disabled child."

Mr. Tom Brinsko
Former President/CEO
YMCA of the Greater Twin Cities
(A dad like us)

"Dads Like Us" fills a critical void in information currently available to fathers raising a child with a disability. It offers encouragement and advice in a down-to-earth manner, simply and calmly addressing practical areas of parenting and being human.

"For dads who often get overlooked (and) sometimes feel unsure about their role in their child's life, this book is both necessary and a breath of fresh air!"

Barbra Holian
Retired Community Rehabilitation Provider

"This book will benefit many dads raising children with disabilities and special needs."

Tammy Larsen, LPN
Author, MarvelousLightBooks.com

"Millions of parents in our country are raising special needs children, myself included. Most dads experience that journey alone, stumbling from one crisis to the next...(this book) has helped me reflect on my own experiences as a special needs father. I wish I had read it fifty years ago!"

Tom Wilson, Ph.D.
Retired Educator
(From the Foreword)

Dads Like Us

*Raising a Child
with Disabilities*

Steve Harris

Did You Know?

• 1 out of 10 American families is raising a child with a disability. (AfterSchool Alliance)

• About 1 in 6 children ages 3-17 in the United States—approximately 17% of that population—is developmentally disabled. (Centers for Disease Control).

• The most common forms of disabilities in newborns are heart defects, neural tube defects and Down syndrome. (World Health Organization)

• Over 760,000 people in the U.S. are currently living with cerebral palsy. 65% are under the age of 18. (Birth Injury Center)

• Preterm (premature) birth affects about 1 of every 10 infants born in the United States each year, putting them at risk of developmental disabilities. (Centers for Disease Control)

• 7.3 million students in the United States (about 15% of all public-school students) receive special education services. (National Center for Education Statistics)

• Approximately 500,000 children become blind every year—one every minute. (Global Initiative)

• On average 380 children in the U.S. are injured every day in traffic crashes. (National Highway Traffic Safety Administration)

ALSO BY STEVE HARRIS

"Lanesboro, Minnesota"

Riverplace Press, 2018

DADS LIKE US

Email: SteveHarrisDLU@gmail.com

ISBN: Print: 979-8-9891917-0-3
ISBN: EBook: 979-8-9891917-1-0

Published by

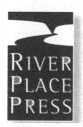

40274 Diamond Lake St.
Aitkin, MN 56431
218.851.4843

www.riverplacepress.com
chip@riverplace-mn.com

RiverPlace Press is distinctive in guiding authors through the maze of specialized publishing options, with personalized service.

This project is made possible, in part, by the Five Wings Arts Council Individual Artist Grant Award with funding from the McKnight Foundation.

McKNIGHT FOUNDATION

FIVE WINGS
ARTS COUNCIL

To

Matthew and Andrew,

my sons.

Special in every way.

TABLE OF CONTENTS

FOREWORD

I have never met Steve Harris, but I have heard wonderful things about him from a mutual friend. That mutual friend called, suggesting that I write the foreword to Mr. Harris' book, written about his experiences raising two special needs sons. I immediately agreed to read and reflect on this literary work, as I, too, have spent more than five decades parenting my own special needs son.

While reading the first page, I was captivated. By the end of page two, I knew a few things about the man. He is an intelligent, authentic, articulate, savvy guy who knows how to write. He is a story teller. He is thoughtful and he cleverly weaves words together to engage the reader. After two pages, I was hooked.

There are millions of parents in our country who are raising special needs children, myself included. Each of us is on our own journey, struggling with feelings of guilt, confusion, anger, sadness, and pride, in addition to our other life challenges. We find it easy to be drawn into the vortex of colliding priorities: how to raise a special child in a "normal" family, how to feel about our other children, how to develop life, work, family balance and much more. Most dads experience that journey alone, stumbling from one crisis to the next.

Mr. Harris, having recognized these realities, has managed to wrestle all of the conflicting priorities into a thoughtful, cogent, carefully organized and cleverly written manuscript that has helped me reflect on my own experiences as a special needs father. I wish I had read this book fifty years ago.

As an educator of some forty-seven years I found myself in envy of Steve Harris, as he has organized the chaos of loving and raising two special needs sons into a primer for dads like us.

This book should be required reading for all dads of special needs children, as well as educators, young men and women studying to be teachers, medical professionals, social workers, law enforcement officers, emergency room workers and court officials.

Thank you, Steve Harris, for your gift to all dads like us.

Thomas F. Wilson, Ph.D. *Retired Educator*

PREFACE

The Book I Needed

The day couldn't be starting better, a New England fall morning framed by gold leaves and royal blue sky that looks like it fell off a calendar. My wife, Pam, and I barely have time to notice, though, as we rush out the front door of our Worcester, Massachusetts, apartment, suitcase in hand. We're hurrying for a good reason. Pam is nine months pregnant and started having contractions just before sunrise. We're on our way to a "birth-day" party!

Our check-in at Hahneman Hospital goes smoothly. The front-desk staff and nurses seem happy, chatty even, for this early Monday morning. Within minutes Pam is lying in bed, eager to start the breathing and focal-point tips we learned in pre-natal classes. By mid-morning, with the contractions growing stronger, nurses push her wheeled-bed towards the delivery room. Wearing paper scrubs and a goofy grin, camera in hand, I eagerly follow behind, feeling like a kid ready to open the world's best Christmas present.

I find a spot at the foot of Pam's bed and give a friendly nod to the delivery-doc as he arrives. His initial exam reveals the baby is butt-first breech but no one seems too alarmed. Then—suddenly—I see the doctor's back stiffen. "We have spina bifida here," he says.

Spina bifida. I'd never heard the term. (It would take me days to learn how to pronounce it.) I look down at the baby—a boy, I see—and notice a quarter-sized patch of dark skin at the base of his spine that looks like a bruise on a peach in a grocery store bin. I quickly dismiss it. How can that little birth mark be a problem? C'mon, everybody, let's get back to happy!

That's not going to happen. As the baby fully emerges (Matthew, "Gift of God," is the name we've chosen) a nurse quickly whisks him over to a small, brightly-lit table. He still hasn't taken a breath. With Matthew's 6-pound, 12-ounce body turning a blueish-gray, a second nurse presses a black rubber mask over his mouth and starts CPR. Our baby finally gasps for air but instead of hearing the healthy, loud cry we'd expected and wanted, what emerges is a weak, clogged gurgle. I put down my camera.

Another nurse approaches me. (The room is suddenly crawling with them, it seems.) "Mr. Harris," she whispers, "do you want me to call for a priest?" At first her question puzzles me, then stings like a face-slap. Apparently they think this is all going to be over very quickly.

Still another nurse catches my eye. If it was happy I wanted, I'd found it. Even through her mask I can see her smiling. Beaming, almost. The crisis unfolding in front of us is somehow energizing her. What in the world is she thinking, I wonder? She decides to tell us. "What a coincidence!" she blurts out to no one in particular. "I'm taking a grad class on spina bifida!" The fact that she seems giddy about it leaves me confused and angry. I decide to just ignore her.

The doctor walks up to me. "The wound on your baby's lower back is leaking spinal fluid and needs immediate surgery to close," he says. "The next twenty-four hours will be critical." Nurses carefully wrap a cloth bandage around Matthew's middle, lift him onto another gurney, and quickly wheel him out of the room. Pam lies in her bed, eyes wide and crying. I stand frozen, staring. This birth-day party has officially become a train wreck.

As a nurse wheels Pam out of the delivery room, I once again follow behind, walking slower this time. We're led to a small, stark room, and left alone, Pam in bed still crying, me sitting next to her in a straight-backed wooden chair. Suddenly the door swings open. In walks Nurse Smiley carrying a thick book. "Hi, there," she says, almost casually. "You know that class I'm taking on spina bifida? This is the textbook. I thought you might like to read it." She reaches across Pam's bed to hand it to me.

I stare at her and brush the book aside. A textbook on spina bifida? Are you kidding me? No, I don't want to read it. What I want to do is throw it at her. Sensing my coldness, she stops smiling (finally), and walks out the door.

I needed something at that moment. Maybe I did need a book. But not that one.

* * * * * * * * * *

What *do* parents need when they first learn their child is disabled? What words help in those first minutes, hours, and days? I've thought about that many times over the years, especially when I remember that nurse and the book she tried to give me.

Over time I began reading articles and books about raising a child with special needs. While helpful, I noticed the majority were written by moms. I began to wonder: is it different for fathers? What do dads need to hear? Would a book for fathers, written by a dad who has gone through this experience himself, be helpful? I'd been a writer through school and in my first jobs. Should I write that book? Forty years later, I'll give it a try.

But who was I to write it? I certainly "qualify" but I don't consider myself an expert. Nor would I claim to be the example to follow. My long journey has had lots of ups-and-downs. Facing those realities actually made me want to write even more. I wanted to write the book I needed— a practical, honest and helpful book for dads facing the unique challenge of raising a child with disabilities. I envisioned a book that would help those dads, and the people who care about them.

I hope you find this book worth your time. If it isn't, put it down. Dads like us have enough to think about and do. Sometimes just helping our kids get through their day—and getting through our own—is about all we can handle. Or, you may not feel like reading a book like this. On many days we'd like to just ignore all this "disability" and "special needs" stuff. The challenges are hard enough—why spend time dwelling on them? I've been there. Some dads go a step further. They think about running away from it all. I tried that, too.

Many, if not most, dads are independent (think stubborn) when it comes to our kids. Faced with tough stuff we're tempted to pull in, put up walls, and just try to grit it out on our own. That may work for some, but not for many. Learning from others can make our journeys a bit easier. I hope this book does that for you.

This short book won't have all the answers. Far from it. Think of it as a starting point, a beginning. The thoughts in it will be simple, the chapters brief. This isn't a time for textbooks.

Your personal journey deserves respect. What you have gone through, and will go through in days to come, has your name on it, no one else's. Your child's story, your family's story, your own story is yours alone. No one should ever say, "I know what you're going through." They don't. I don't. Only you do.

While that's true, dads do share common feelings, places, encounters and experiences. We'll focus on those in this book. Feelings like sadness, anger, and isolation. Places like hospitals, clinics and schools. People like doctors, nurses and teachers. We'll briefly touch on common challenges as well, like how to balance "normal" life (including marriage and career) with parenting realities far from normal.

Feel free to share this book with others. The life we live can be hard to talk about. This book might help jump-start needed conversations. Who else might want (or need) to read this? Your wife, spouse or partner, certainly. Parents and siblings, grandparents, extended family members, close friends. Key work colleagues, perhaps. Doctors, nurses, therapists, social workers, and other people you regularly encounter. Pastors, chaplains, spiritual leaders. Helping others know your world better can help you, and your whole family.

At book's end you'll find a "tool-box" with some brief practical helps, including a getting-started medical "glossary," contact info for key support organizations, suggestions for additional reading, long-term planning ideas, and prompts to help you think deeper about topics we've introduced. I hope that information is helpful to you, at the right time.

Dad, you're on a path that will change your life. Know that many days will be difficult and tiring. A few will be overwhelming. Find comfort and courage in the fact that you've already made it through the first days, some of the hardest of all. Also, the fact that you're reading this book shows your willingness to face difficult issues. That says something very positive about you already.

Many days ahead will also be wonderful. Extraordinary, even. Moments and memories await you that only a father can truly appreciate, the kind that will make you incredibly thankful to be a dad.

And a dad like us.

Introduction

Welcome to the Club

This book is for dads, but not just any dads. It's a book for fathers who have a child who is disabled and has special needs. This is a book for dads like us.

Like it or not, you and I belong to a club. Groucho said he didn't want to join a club that would take someone like him for a member. Somehow that fits us. This isn't a club we ever wanted—or expected—to join.

I was beyond thrilled when I learned that Pam was pregnant. The last thing I wanted to think about was the possibility that our baby might have "problems." I wasn't naïve. I knew some kids are born with disabilities (or "birth defects," to use that old, ugly phrase). I had a distant relative, a couple of friends, and at least one work colleague who had children with special needs. I felt sorry for those kids and their parents—when I thought about them at all. But I wanted no part of that scary world. Besides, the odds were in our favor. What, me worry? So I didn't.

But, it happened. You and I are in this club. We know if we qualify. We don't got to show you no stinkin' badges. We live in the house down the street where the short yellow school bus pulls into the driveway.

There are more of us than you might think. Every year more than three million children are born in this country with a serious disability. Sadly, nearly half will pass away before their fifth birthday. The others survive but face unpredictable futures—physically, mentally, emotionally, and socially. So do their dads. Three million is a lot of kids. And a lot of dads, too.

Maybe you joined the club recently when your child was born. You found out right away that he or she was disabled. Your head might still be spinning. Maybe your child's diagnosis is not even fully known yet. What you do know is that all of this is unexpected, unsettling and frightening.

It helps to know other people feel confused and fearful about this, too. No one expected this. Not your wife, your partner, your siblings, your parents, your child's grandparents, your friends, no one. Other people who know and care about you are struggling to process what's happening to your child, your family, and to you. No one knows exactly what to say. Many end up saying nothing at all.

Maybe your child's disability became real in a different way. You got the news in a hospital after a sudden illness or tragic accident. You woke up one morning in one world. You went to bed that night in another. Your life will never be the same.

Sometimes the diagnosis arrives slowly. You go through months, maybe even years, of nagging doubts, worries, medical tests, second opinions, and sleepless nights. It feels like you're falling down a flight of stairs in slow motion. Then—in a doctor's office, or by letter or phone call—you get the news. That dark storm-cloud that had been hanging off in the distance finally arrives in full force.

My son Matthew's delivery-room shock was followed by that first surgery and dozens more in his first years. He remained in intensive care for nearly a year. When finally released he came home to a room long past the fun nursery stage. Out went the crib; in came a hospital bed. Out went the comfy rocking chair where we planned to sing lullabies; in its place stood two tall oxygen tanks. The butterfly mobile over his bed was removed to make room for an IV drip-pole.

We were thrilled to have Matthew home but those follow-up surgeries and recurring pneumonias sent him (and us) back to the hospital frequently. Most frightening were his unexplained and unpredictable "apneic spells." As many as a dozen times a day he would suddenly stop breathing, from 20-30 seconds to 2-3 minutes. Each spell might could potentially end his life, doctors told us, so quiet panic set in every time we sensed one coming on.

We'd immediately start CPR, subconsciously holding our own breath until he took one of his own. While most spells happened at home, he also had them in his car seat, in a grocery store aisle, a church pew, at McDonalds, and more than a few on a playground. Turning on the vacuum cleaner seemed to bring them on, too. Go figure.

The news arrived differently with our second son, Andrew. After Matthew's birth, for obvious reasons, it was years before we could ever think or talk about having more children. Matthew's daily care-needs were an obvious barrier. A second was the fear that a second baby might also be disabled. Through genetic counselling at St. Paul's Gillette

Hospital we learned our chances of having a second child with spina bifida were very low. Thankfully, Matthew's health stabilized and his apneic spells decreased. Eight years later we celebrated Pam's new pregnancy with cautious optimism.

Andrew Todd Harris filled his delivery room with those loud cries we'd missed with his older brother. Our healthy newborn came home the next day (this really happens?). Even with Matthew's long-term special needs, our future finally held some hope.

Over time, though, we noticed Andrew lagging behind in key benchmarks. His first steps, beyond cute-and-clumsy, resulted in numerous falls and a few stitches. His speech was garbled. Global developmental delay, they'd call it today. His pediatrician ordered extensive tests, including a brain scan. Two weeks later I sat with my three-year-old in a neurologist's office. "The MRI reveals white spots on Andrew's brain," she said. "Your son has cerebral palsy."

I sat there, staring and silent. Again. The doctor handed me a brochure (at least it wasn't a textbook) and we walked out of the office, Andrew grabbing at my hand and stumbling alongside me. Suddenly, in the flash of a moment, everything felt very different. Our hopes for a normal child had ended. Life felt more uncertain and frightening than ever.

The "news" we dads receive might come in familiar words. Cerebral Palsy. Down Syndrome. Muscular Dystrophy. Cystic Fibrosis. Dwarfism. Autism. Maybe yours arrived in strange words you struggled to pronounce. It doesn't really matter. What you do know is that this is your child they're talking about. This is the moment you didn't expect. This is the news you never wanted to hear.

More than forty years later—embarrassing to admit, but true—I still have do-over fantasies. I picture myself back in Matthew's delivery room. This time, everything goes right. A healthy baby is surrounded by happy people. My Andrew fantasy takes place in that neurologist's office. "Your son is just fine," the doctor says with a reassuring smile. "He'll grow out of this." Fantasies are fun but quickly and painfully evaporate. Then it's back to reality.

We know the only choice is to move on. But hard questions travel with us. Will my child have anything close to a normal life? Will they fit in at school? Will they have friends? Will they be able to work at a job? Will they fall in love and get married? The most personal question of all lingers, too: how will I as their father handle all of this?

Dad, however and whenever you arrived, welcome to the club.

1

Shock

The first feelings are no feelings. It won't last long. While it does, go easy on yourself—and on others. Find (and create) places and moments to stop and catch your breath. Lean on the people who are offering help. You need them.

A person injured in a severe accident is at risk of going into shock. Their blood pressure drops, breathing grows shallow, they might pass out. Physical shock is serious and can even be life-threatening.

Emotional shock is serious, too. That's when someone is suddenly thrust into an unexpected, frightening, overwhelming situation. Emotional shock doesn't have physical symptoms. The person going through it, and those around him or her, may not even be aware it's happening. But emotional shock is real and has an impact on the way a person feels, thinks and acts.

When a dad discovers there's "something wrong" with his child he might experience emotional shock. He may appear disconnected and distant, but exactly the opposite is true. He's on mental overload. So many emotions bombard him all at once—surprise, fear, and worry, to name just three—that he shuts down. That's actually a good thing. Like a surge protector on a computer during a lightning storm, emotional shock protects a human brain from being overwhelmed by too many feelings.

When my son, Matthew, was born, I whiplashed from mountaintop ecstasy to near-panic in less than five minutes. The voices of the delivery room doctor and nurses sounded like the *wah-wah-wah* of Charlie Brown's teacher. "When I was told my daughter was disabled," remembers one parent, "it was like somebody placed a black bag over my head." I can relate to that. Maybe you can, too.

In those first hours, I needed to fight my way out of my emotional shock. Our newborn, barely clinging to life, was headed to a second hospital for emergency surgery. My wife, Pam, dealing with her own physical and emotional trauma, experienced multiple fainting spells. I needed to be strong for both of them. I wanted to be Superman. It felt like I was wearing kryptonite underwear.

That's how emotional shock hit me. How was it for you? What did it "feel" like to "not feel?" What do you remember about those first hours and days with your child? What helps us best function during that period?

First, know what's happening. Don't be surprised when you experience this. Certainly don't feel embarrassed or guilty. Merging a car onto a highway can be the most dangerous part of a long trip. When our child's disability is revealed, we're in merge mode. Know it, accept it, and—as best you can—work your way through these early moments, one foot in front of another.

Second, know that communications can be challenging. In the delivery room you probably had a list of people to contact with "five fingers, five toes" good news. That's all changed. In the first hours, days and weeks after your child's disability is confirmed, you might still feel obligated to contact people. I found it difficult—impossible at times— to do that, vacillating between pushing people away and wanting to vent. I'm thankful for gracious and forgiving family and friends who gave me room to do both.

It can even be hard when people reach out to you. Within days after Matthew was born, I received phone calls from relatives I hadn't heard from in years. I even had a few from people I'd never met, including a young dad from Cape Cod whose son had spina bifida, who called to say, "...my kid is doing great; you're going to be fine." That's all happening when you're still in a mental fog. Not easy.

People will want to tell you things. People will want to know things. Texts and apps can help with that. Mainly, take it slow, do the best you can, don't feel guilty, and trust kind people to be understanding. They most normally are.

Third, find spaces to process emotional shock. Depending on your child's medical situation, lots of information comes at you quickly. Doctors explain diagnoses, treatment plans, medications, and possible surgeries. Nurses orient you to new places, procedures and protocols.

Other people show up as well, including therapists and social workers. All those people, and all they're telling you, can often blur together. Add normal daily duties to all that (caring for your other children, perhaps, job deadlines, and other family matters), and it's no wonder you're on overload.

Our heads may be spinning. We need time and spaces where we can begin to process all of that. Thankfully, I found one the day Matthew was born, a candle-lit chapel off the lobby of the hospital where he'd have his surgery. The silence of that small space drew me in. I sat in the quiet for maybe five minutes, long enough to take a few deep breaths and whisper a simple prayer. It helped. In your first days, look for places and moments like that. If you don't easily find them, make a few of your own.

Fourth, let others help. Shock can be isolating, and its timing could not be worse. This is a time when we need people. We need their presence. We need their practical help (meals, transportation, childcare for other kids, perhaps). Alone time can be helpful; staying isolated isn't good for anyone.

Near midnight of that first day, with Matthew still in surgery, I was sitting alone in a waiting room. Familiar voices suddenly echoed down the hallway and in walked Dave, Jim, Kim, and Tom, four college-age friends from church. They were carrying two big pizzas. At first I cringed, thinking it was just easier to be alone. That's not what I needed. We talked a bit, ate a bit, shared quick hugs. They didn't stay long but it was good to have them there. When people show up in your life, accept them as gifts. When people ask how they can help, let them. It's good for them and for you.

Fifth, know that shock won't last long. In a few hours or days, perhaps—on your clock, no one else's—your mental fog will lift. You'll return to normal. (A "new" normal that is.) Renewed courage and strength will kick in. Soon you'll be ready to face the days ahead. As difficult as it can be that's what dads like us need to do.

Sadness

You will feel sad. You'll know grief. Why? Because you've lost something. But know that you've found something, too.

Traffic was light as I drove across town to the hospital where Matthew would have his first surgery. Approaching a crosswalk I had to stop for a group of elementary school kids headed to a nearby playground. A teacher was carefully herding her little cats but a few stragglers broke ranks and approached my front bumper. A little girl with reddish curls looked directly at me with a big smile. Just a very ordinary moment in what was for those kids a very ordinary day.

I looked at the little girl and tried to return her smile, but couldn't. Huge tears suddenly blurred my vision until I couldn't see her at all. I brushed my hand across my face, grabbed for my sunglasses, and drove away, hoping she hadn't noticed. Where did *that* come from? Stress from the entire morning was one obvious factor. But it felt deeper than that. At least I was coming out of my emotional fog and was feeling something. But what exactly?

Pretty simple, really. I was feeling sad. For the first time, while watching those kids, I realized that my little boy—if he does live—will be different. There *is* "something wrong" with him. He will be disabled. He will have special needs. He will not be "normal." He will never casually walk to a playground with a group of classmates. Maybe he'll never go to a regular school at all. Maybe he'll never know an "ordinary" day. That's why the tears. I was feeling sad.

Dads like us don't easily admit we feel sad about our child. We rarely, if ever, talk about it. But we do feel it. Sadness shows up at different times with different intensities. Sometimes it has the sting of a wasp bite. Other times it drapes over us like a dark, wet blanket. But we do feel sad.

People feel sad when they lose something. What have we lost? Think of the months before your baby was born. It was a time of preparing for the new arrival, baby showers, stocking the nursery, all of that. Most of the attention had been on the mom-to-be, rightfully so, but dads get into that, too. We try to imagine our baby. Boy or girl? Hair color? Who will they look like? We're already anticipating birthday parties, Christmas mornings, the sheer joy of being a dad. We can't wait to be in that delivery room holding our child for the first time!

Then, for dads like us, it doesn't happen like that. Our "normal" baby doesn't show up. In a sense, you lose that child. Your dreams die. That's why you feel sad. That's why you know grief.

What do we do with that? Here are some points to consider.

Express sadness in ways that fit you. You might shed some tears. You might not. You might just feel numb. Maybe you'll get a migraine. Sadness can trigger flashes of temper. Some people just get very quiet. People might think you aren't feeling anything. You know better.

Sadness doesn't disappear. Sometimes people talk about "working through grief" like it's a 5K run with a finish line. That's not how it goes. It's more like an airplane circling overhead that never seems to land, or what others describe as "the Lazy Susan of grief." One dad, now in his 80s, says that after his daughter was born with severe disabilities he and his wife "...came home, went into our bedroom, and wept. Off and on, we've been weeping ever since."

Sadness changes. Four decades later, I still feel sad about my sons' disabilities. In early years, my grief felt like I was dragging around a 200-pound suitcase everywhere I went. It made everything harder. Sadness lightens over time. Today I'd describe it as a 20-pound backpack, still there, cumbersome at times, but manageable. Some days are "heavier" than others—birthdays, holidays, anniversaries. Even good times can bring twinges of grief. Never easy, but you learn to manage it the best you can.

Sadness is eased by finding new joys. Dads like us do "lose" something valuable when we learn about our child's disabilities. We lose the child who never showed up. We lose the expectations and dreams we had surrounding that child. But we found something, too. That makes all the difference.

I first discovered that healing truth in the hours after Matthew's initial surgery. The doctor came out to tell me my newborn son had survived the operation. "He's stable and breathing on his own," he said. "He's not out of the woods yet, but he's hanging in there. Your baby boy is quite a fighter!"

A few minutes later they let me see Matthew in the recovery room. Tubes and wires snaked everywhere around his little body. Nurses buzzed in and out, monitors were beeping, it felt like choreographed chaos. But I only saw one thing. A newborn baby. My son. I saw a person, a small, vulnerable person, with scruffs of dark hair and big brown eyes (like his mommy's) looking right at me. I leaned down and squeezed my fingers into his covered isolette to gently stroke his arm and touch his teeny fingers. "The doctor says you're a little fighter, Matthew!" I whisper to him. "I'm your dad. I'm here with you. I love you. I am so proud of you!"

I found something in those moments I would never lose. I found my son, Matthew, a "gift from God." How could I not love this kid? What we find, even in our sadness, is a priceless gift that overwhelms any loss. Another dad wisely put it like this. "There comes a point where you must stop mourning the child who never arrived and start celebrating the child who is there."

We can be honest about our sadness. We can admit it is real, it hurts, and it lingers. What also remains—on a much higher level—is our precious child, the amazing little boy or girl who did show up. May the celebration of that life begin and never end!

Anger

You'll feel angry and might even lose your temper a time or two. Be careful, though. While anger can be understandable and even useful at times, it is also powerful and can leave a mark. Manage it wisely.

When dads like us learn our child is disabled, we'll be in shock for a bit. We'll feel a sadness that lingers. We can also get mad as hell. Why do we get angry? That's complicated. We're angry that our child is disabled. We're angry that this is happening to our family. And honestly we are angry that this is happening to us.

Anger often wears disguises. Sometimes it's quiet, a seething, slow burn. Other times—especially when ignited by too much stress and not enough sleep—it gets loud and tempers flare. Anger can turn inward, too, transforming into a dark, paralyzing depression.

Where do people see our anger? Lots of places. In a doctor's office, at a teacher's meeting, on a phone call with a social worker. Sadly and stupidly, we might even lash out at home at the people closest to us. Anger is unpredictable.

Hospitals can often become a stage for angry parents. In the movie *Terms of Endearment*, a mom frustrated by delays in getting pain meds for her sick daughter gets very angry. She tries keeping it together but ends up screaming at the nurses: "Give her the shot!" Meds arrive, mom calms down, peace is (mostly) restored. I've been there. Maybe you have, too. Maybe you will be.

My hospital eruption happened years ago in an ER. Matthew and I arrived on a Sunday afternoon after he had been running a high fever all weekend. A nurse took us to a cubicle, hooked him up to the monitors and told me a doctor would be right in. A half-hour later, no doctor had shown up. Matthew's oxygen levels began to drop and monitor alarms started ringing. I'm sure they'll be in now, I figured.

Nope, still no doctor. I walked out to the Nurses Station. "My son isn't doing well," I said. The nurse looked at me coldly. "The doctor will be right there," she answered. I thanked her, hurried back, and found Matthew thrashing back-and-forth in his bed so violently that he had rubbed the skin on his elbows red-raw. Another five minutes passed. Alarms still ringing. Still no doctor. Back to the Nurses Station. "Can someone check on my son?!" I asked, more firmly this time. Another icy glare. "We're doing the best we can, sir. It's busy here today." Frustrated, I raced back to Matthew's room. His O2 numbers were lower. My blood pressure was higher. Alarms kept ringing.

Suddenly I felt strangely philosophical. My son is sick, I reasoned. Machines monitor his condition. Those machines have alarms. When there's a problem, the alarm rings. But if an alarm rings and no one responds to it, is it really an alarm? (Kind of like that famous tree falling in that forest). If it isn't an alarm, what is it? Why, merely an irritating, meaningless noise. What can you do with an irritating, meaningless noise? That's easy. Turn it off.

So I did. Slowly and methodically I walked around Matthew's hospital room and began turning off all the monitor alarms—oxygen, heart monitor, blood pressure. The machines were working, but all the alarms stopped. The room got very quiet.

I felt calm. I wasn't, of course. I was angry. Very angry. Scary angry. My plug-pulling stunt did get attention. A nurse quickly rushed into the room. She was angry, too. "What do you think you're doing?" she demanded. "My son needs a doctor," I said firmly. "If alarms don't get somebody's attention, what will?" She quickly re-plugged the alarms. Next a doctor walked in. (I think he was mad, too.) He glanced at Matthew and ordered x-rays and a blood draw. Within 30 minutes my son was diagnosed with a serious pneumonia. IV antibiotics were started and over the next four days he fought—and beat—an infection that could have ended his life.

What did we learn here? My son was sick. I felt he was being ignored. I got angry. I did stupid stuff. I'm thankful Matthew got the treatment he needed and hugely grateful he recovered. I'm not happy with how I acted. I'm embarrassed, actually. But not ashamed.

Dads like us get angry. Not often, hopefully, but it happens.
Tensions erupt. Voices get raised. We might lose our temper. We might
have conflicts with a few doctors, nurses, therapists, maybe a teacher or
two. It even happens with our spouses or partners, relatives and friends.
Those aren't our best moments. "Speak when you're angry," it's been said,
"and you'll make the best speech you'll ever regret." That can happen.

In her book *My Year of Magical Thinking*, Joan Didion describes the
time her daughter was hospitalized with a serious illness. After one
particularly stressful day, the girl's father got very angry with the doctors.
That shouldn't surprise us, Didion writes. "It's not normal for a father to
see his child in need outside of his control." Parents, especially fathers,
are wired to fix anything that threatens their child. When they can't fix
it, they get worried, frustrated—and angry.

Anger can damage others; it can also damage us. "A heart stained
in anger grows weak and grows bitter," says a John Prine lyric. How do
we keep that from happening? A story about a volcano provides one
possible strategy. The biggest eruption of all time happened on the Island
of Krakatoa in 1883 with the destructive force of 13,000 atomic bombs.
The explosion was heard 2,000 miles away! Why so massive? Scientists
theorize that throughout its long-existence Krakatoa had never had
"small" eruptions. Pressure just kept building. When it finally blew, it
really blew!

The lesson for us? Letting off steam in small doses can help. There
are simple ways to do that. Some people jog, others vent to a trusted
friend, maybe a long walk (with a few solitary screams) works for you.
Whatever helps.

There are times when dads like us *should* get angry. I get angry
when I see group home staff watching TV instead of doing their work.
(One afternoon while visiting Matthew I found staff watching a show—
with residents present—about a group home worker who murdered
people where she worked. I mean, come on.) I got mad the day I found
myself cleaning a dirty bathroom at Andrew's group home. I also lost it
when he fell out of bed in the middle of the night and laid on the floor
for three hours. When a scheduled bus failed to pick him up after his
Walmart work shift, leaving him sitting alone on a dark street, I got angry.
Yes, stuff happens, honest mistakes get made, no one is perfect. But there

are times when dads should get angry. Anger can even be productive. It can motivate needed advocacy. It holds people accountable for our child's care. All good things.

Anger happens in dads like us. When it does, handle with care.

The Parade

*A parade will march through your child's life. Each
person marching in it is important, many are priceless,
a few annoying, a handful, extraordinary. See the whole
group as a team that's there to help your child...and you.*

Who doesn't love a parade? Marching bands, colorful floats, fire
trucks, clowns, balloons. Dads like us watch a different parade, though.
This one is made up of all the people who come into our child's life.
Doctors, nurses, therapists, special education teachers, social workers,
case managers, personal care attendants, group home staff, school
principals, psychologists and counselors, transportation workers, and
more. A very big parade.

Most of the time that parade flows smoothly. Then there are times
when it has all the coordination of a junior high cheerleading squad.
During emergencies this parade speeds up. It can slow down, too, and
frustrating gaps appear. When long-time marchers leave that parade you
feel sad and a bit lost. Many days you've had enough and just want the
whole thing to end. But this parade keeps moving and that's actually a
very good thing.

Your parade begins when your child's disability is diagnosed. It takes
time for us to get a handle on all that's going on. Being dads, we may try
to organize and even control it. It's better, especially at first, to stay back,
ask questions, and listen. There's a lot to take in.

Don't get lost in the crowd, though. That can happen to dads.
Professionals have a tendency to ignore fathers, assuming the mom is lead
caretaker. Sometimes we bring it on ourselves by keeping our distance.
Whatever the reasons, it does happen. A friend of mine who is disabled
says her father "...ended up in no man's land" when she was born. During
Matthew's first weeks in the hospital, I did notice doctors
communicating more directly to my wife than to me. I figured it was a

planned time-saver—talk to one parent, assume they'll tell the other. But I needed doctor-facetime, too. Don't hesitate to push to the front of the parade, Dad. You are needed there!

Here are good things to remember as you watch your child's parade.

This parade is for your child. They are the center, the star, and the reason for all that's happening. Those "marchers" are there to help your child. That's what this is about. Nothing is more important.

Sometimes the parade feels overwhelming. People will be there when you want them to be—and even when you don't. It can feel suffocating. When it reaches that point, step back, take a breath, (maybe take a walk), and give yourself some space. We all need that at times.

This parade moves. I once lived near a southern Minnesota town so small that the only way they could have a parade was for it to stay in one place and have spectators walk around it. A "stand-still parade," they called it. Your child's "parade" is *not* a stand-still parade! It's always moving. People march in and out of it all the time.

That can be good. Some "marchers" can be difficult to work with; when they move on, you're not unhappy. But most of the time seeing people leave *is* hard. Your child—and you—get comfortable with certain doctors, nurses, therapists, and teachers. You're pleased with their work. They have bonded with your child. They communicate well with you. Then, life happens. They move, change jobs, get promoted. They leave your child's parade, and that can be hard for everybody.

Beth was Matthew's first school-based physical therapist. Her smiles, hugs and caring spirit were gifts to him, and to our family. His face lit up every time he saw her. It was a very sad day at our house when we learned Beth was leaving. Who can ever replace her, I wondered? Those goodbyes happen in our parades. It doesn't get easier. You get wiser, though. You learn to appreciate people without getting too attached or dependent on them. You are grateful for their time in your child's life, then look forward to new people who will—in their own unique ways—make a positive impact as well.

Find your spot. Watch your parade closely. Meet the people marching in it. Make sure—as much as possible—that everything is running smoothly and that everyone is on the same page regarding treatment plans and goals. Along with your child's mom, of course, and perhaps a few other key people, you are the only one who is with this parade from its beginning. No one knows it better.

Dads need to help lead their child's parade. That may not be a natural fit for you, but you can ask questions, help define priorities, and monitor progress. Another practical role dads can play is "trainer." Our child's parade will see lots of people come and go. When new marchers arrive, don't assume they're fully aware of your child's needs. I once had to stop a new nurse from squirting liquid pain meds into Matthew's mouth; she didn't know he could only receive meds through his stomach tube. Later I worked with group home staff to define protocols for his apneic spells. I certainly wasn't the expert. We needed to work together. But dads need to play a key role in guiding this parade.

Enjoy happy surprises. A parade isn't always predictable. That can be unnerving. It can also be a good thing. Take Joe Parrish, for example.

After a family move Matthew needed a new elementary school. We checked out many, but the best fit required a two-hour daily commute. A bus wasn't available so the proposed plan was to use a taxi. I was very skeptical and raised an obvious question: how is a taxi driver going to handle a medically-fragile rider like Matthew? That driver turned out to be Joe Parrish, a tall, thin man in his 50s with a curly-grey Bob Ross-perm, a relaxed, easy smile, and a cool confidence that he could handle Matthew just fine. Singing country-western tunes daily with Joe proved to be a highlight in my son's life. Joe joining our parade was a surprise—and a joy—we didn't expect. Keep your eyes open for your own.

See your parade as a team. It might seem disorganized at times. It may look like disconnected people all doing their own thing. But it really needs to work as a unit. It won't be perfect. Every parade will have things to fix, tweak, and improve as it moves along. But with everyone working together, it can reach its goal: to help your child—the star of the parade—reach his or her full potential. Who wouldn't love a parade like that?

Doctors

Doctors will play a major role in your child's life. Be thankful for each one. See them as unique men and women with personal strengths and weaknesses. Respect their expertise and experience, but don't be intimidated by them.

Your child is the star of the parade. But someone else gets lots of attention. Doctors. That's understandable, because more than anyone else, doctors guide your child's medical care. In consultation with dad and mom, doctors call the shots and make the big decisions. Those men and women in the white coats definitely help run the entire parade.

We respect doctors and are thankful for all they do for our kids. They are unique in ages, personalities, and backgrounds, with varied communication styles. Some are outgoing. (They like to wave in the parade). Others are quiet, low-key, even shy. Our challenge is to work well with all those different people, with all those varied factors, in often stressful circumstances. Because they're in a "power position," that can also make them intimidating.

Remember, doctors are just people. They put on those white coats one arm at a time. They are men and women dealing with their own good and bad days, marriage tensions, financial pressures, and parenting issues themselves, perhaps.

We see all this played out in their varied work styles. Some doctors are very clinical and come across as insensitive. Maybe that's a self-protection mechanism in their highly-stressful jobs. Whatever the reason, a doctor's coldness can be unsettling. After Matthew had a bad week of frequent and frightening apneic spells, I asked his doctor, "why does this happen?" "Brain-damaged people do all kinds of things," he answered brusquely. Gee, thanks, Doc. My trophy for medical rudeness, though, goes to the oral surgeon who—upon meeting Andrew for an initial consult—glanced at my son in his wheelchair, turned to me, and asked, "So, what's wrong with him?" End of consult.

My experience—yours too, I hope—is that caring doctors far outnumber the icy ones. Dr. Vicki was the first physician we worked with during Matthew's intensive care stay. A bright, friendly, energetic intern in her mid-20s, she became a stabilizing rock for us in the stressful first weeks of our baby's life. She sincerely cared about her patient and his parents. Despite her hectic schedule she even joined us for an evening of volleyball and pizza with friends. Hopefully you've had physicians like Dr. Vicki.

She was the first of many outstanding doctors our sons have had. Dr. Giles. Dr. Marshall. Dr. Marker. Dr. Najarian. Dr. Bennett. Dr. Strathy. Dr. Koop. Dr. Moynihan. Dr. Brutlag. Dr. Wagner. Dr. Nance—all special doctors who brought incredible smarts and genuine humanity to our parade. I'm thankful for each one. What names are on your list?

Here are seven brief thoughts to consider when dealing with doctors.

First, trust them. Honor their training, experience and skills. They obviously know more than we do. Trust that they know what they're doing. (If you don't, get that settled right away). Respect the crucial role doctors play in your child's care.

Second, keep them off pedestals. They don't belong there. They probably don't want to be there, either. If they do, well, that needs fixing. Or a new doctor.

Third, communicate well with them. Medical issues with our children get complicated. Doctor-speak gets thick pretty fast. Make sure they provide information in ways that make sense to you. Ask questions. Take notes. Ask nurses to clarify. One of Matthew's doctors sketched little doodles to explain stuff. Whatever works.

Fourth, speak up for your child. You might face tough decisions, especially about medicines and recommended surgeries. Exploring other options and seeking second opinions are always appropriate. Some doctors may take that personally. This isn't about them. It's about getting your child the best care.

Fifth, give respect, expect respect. You might find yourself working with a doctor who doesn't value your input. That's unacceptable. During one especially long and difficult hospital stay for Matthew I requested a care conference with the entire medical team to get everyone on the same page. When one doctor showed up late and began dominating the discussion I respectfully but forcefully spoke up. That wasn't easy, but totally needed. And it helped.

Dad, you're not a casual bystander in all that's happening, you're a key player. Expect to be a respected participant in everything related to your child. Sometimes we need to work around certain doctors. Good nurses can help with that. It might mean waiting for a troublesome physician or two to leave the parade and for better ones to join it. That happens, too.

Sixth, hospital clocks—all medical care?—run on CDT (Central Doctor Time). That means lots of waiting, which can be frustrating. Yes, busy doctors have tight schedules and emergencies happen. Get used to CDT (as much as possible). Give doctors some slack. Fighting it too often will just wear you out.

Seventh, doctors aren't miracle workers. They do the best they can for your child. Most do a great job. Treasure the few who go the extra mile. Doctors aren't gods. As they say, medicine is "practiced." Another doctor put it this way: "Half of what we learned in medical school was probably wrong. We're just not sure which half." We want to think doctors have all the answers. They don't. Another painful reality? Not all medical challenges have happy endings.

The 21st century medical world is experiencing change at laser-speed. Years ago one doctor pretty much handled everything in one patient's care. Today you meet scores of specialists. (I recently had to learn what a "hospitalist" is.) Your child's unique diagnosis and medical needs will determine your doctor "lineup." Learn to be flexible and thankful for the expertise each one brings.

Lots of doctors may march in your parade, but they're all still treating one patient: your child. You have every right to expect the care and treatment he or she receives to be delivered in a thorough, professional, and caring manner. Always. Dads, we cannot and should not ever settle for less.

Nurses

Right behind doctors in our parade come the nurses.
They deserve great respect, too. Wise dads learn from
nurses. The indispensable work they do can sometimes
be overlooked. Be sure to thank them for all they do.

While doctors ride the biggest floats in your child's parade, right behind them come nurses. The care they provide your child, and your family, and you, is crucial. We wouldn't make it without them.

Nurse name tags are alphabet soup: RN, LPN, ICU, ER, VN. You'll probably meet and work with surgical nurses, respiratory nurses, respite care nurses, nurse practitioners, visiting nurses, and more. Titles aren't important; what nurses do is priceless. Most are women (eight out of ten, say recent reports) but you'll work with male nurses, too. Like doctors, each nurse is unique and has his or her own personality and communication styles. Appreciating them and working closely with them is the smart thing to do.

I didn't know many nurses before my sons were born. That changed quickly. Hours after Matthew's difficult arrival, I went to the second hospital for his initial surgery. I was told he was in the NICU, the Neo-Natal Intensive Care Unit, another new name to learn that day. When I found it, I pushed the button for the automatic door and walked right in. Big mistake. A firm hand—belonging to the unit's charge nurse—immediately clamped down on my shoulder, swung me around, and pushed me back out the door.

"No one is allowed in here without being scrubbed and gowned!" the nurse barked, shoving a stiff brush and squeeze-bottle of Betadine into my hand. I felt scolded, defensive and angry. She was doing the right thing, of course, protecting the vulnerable babies in that room—including my own—from possible germs and infections. Her manner stung but her lesson was one I needed to learn.

That tense nurse-encounter was quickly eclipsed by a second. Dutifully scrubbed and gowned, I entered the NICU and wandered a bit before locating "Boy Harris." A smiling nurse approached me, introduced herself, and quickly asked, "Did mom have any time with her new baby?" "Not really," I answered. "They rushed him out of the delivery room pretty fast."

"Let's see what we can do about that," she said, reaching into a nearby cupboard to take out a Polaroid camera. Soon we had our first baby pictures, a bit blurry in those pre-digital days, but very special. "Show these to her," she said, with another smile. "Let her see what a handsome little boy she has!" I did just that. Today—four decades later—those now-faded photos remain a family treasure thanks to one caring and empathetic nurse.

A nurse becomes many things to your child, and to dads like us. Helper, mini-doctor, caregiver, medical translator, friend, counselor, sister, brother, all rolled into one. The world you're entering with your child is complex, complicated, often frightening. Think of your nurse as an experienced tour guide there to help you navigate all that. They know what's going on. They're more accessible than doctors, too. Some nurses, especially those who've been at their jobs for a while, are especially helpful. Later we got to know Nurse Sharon who had been the nurse for Matthew's main doctor for thirty years. She ran that office like a drill sergeant and everything went better because of that. Be thankful for the Nurse Sharons you meet along the way.

Years later Visiting Nurses also joined our parade. At first they came to our home daily to do Matthew's cares and train us to do them ourselves. It felt awkward to have them in our "space," but we adjusted and came to rely heavily on them. Right behind them came Respite Care Nurses who provided much-needed breaks so Pam and I could run errands, enjoy a meal out, or just take a nap. Nurse Toby and others were life-savers for our child and for us. Check out respite care services that might be available for your child.

Nurses provide technical care—giving meds, changing dressings, and the like—but they do much more. Nurses bring a calming presence to stressful situations. They help you believe your child (and you) are going to get through all this. What you're facing with your child is probably your first rodeo—it isn't theirs.

Experienced nurses know there's more than one "patient" present. They'll keep an eye on you, too. "Have you two had anything to eat today?" a nurse might ask. They're not prying; they're looking at the big picture and that includes your whole family.

Matthew's health weakened in his thirties. One of the nurses at his group home knew I was struggling with his decline, especially when he lost his ability to talk. "Matthew needs you to be strong right now," she told me, in a firm but caring voice. "If you have to fake that, just do it. Let him know—more than ever—that you love him and you're with him." I needed that. I took her advice and it made a difference.

Who are the most important people in a child's life when they're hospitalized? Parents, of course. Relatives and close friends, a close second. Right behind them come nurses. That makes it especially hard when we soon realize that nurses, perhaps more than anyone else, move quickly in-and-out of the parade. While they are there—for your child and you—welcome their support and don't forget to let them know how grateful you are for it.

After nearly a year in Intensive Care, Matthew was finally able to come home. It was a day few of us thought we'd ever see. To celebrate that special occasion his nurses threw him a party with a cake, balloons, presents, the whole works. The best part was seeing all of those amazing people in one room. These nurses had cared for him 24/7. They cared for us, too, helping us through an incredibly challenging year. His nurses gave Matthew a gift that day, a hand-painted ceramic plaque with a poem they'd written.

Dear Matthew, you came one day and stole our heart.
But now it is time for us to part.
Now off you go
Home to Mom and Dad.
How lucky we've been to have known such a lad!

Love, All your Nurses.

They felt lucky. We knew we were blessed. Doctors bring the "head" to your child's care. Nurses bring the "heart." What a priceless combination, for our child, and for us.

7

Therapists

Therapists can also be overlooked but shouldn't be. The specialized care and support they provide our child helps in so many ways. Therapists can also help us see our kids—everyone, really—with fresh, new eyes.

A few people in your child's parade march far from the center of attention. That includes therapists. We can be tempted to think of them as "junior varsity" compared to more prominent doctors and specialists. But therapists play an essential role in the lives and development of our kids. Don't let them get lost in your parade!

Depending on your child's diagnosis, special needs, age, and other factors, you'll work with different types of therapists. That happens in hospitals, clinics, schools, sometimes even in your home. There are many different types of therapists: occupational, neurological, speech, mental health, language, and behavioral, to name the most common. (There are nearly half a million physical therapists in the U.S. alone.) The field is large and growing.

My son, Matthew, because of his spina bifida (among other things we'd later learn), was paralyzed from the waist down. He also had weakness and spasticity in his arms and hands. Physical and orthopedic therapists came to his hospital bedside within a few weeks of his birth. Their daily stretching and range-of-motion exercises with him helped keep Matthew's muscles flexible. Although a bit painful for him to do (and for dad to watch) those sessions helped him grow stronger every day.

I mentioned Beth earlier, Matthew's first home-based physical therapist. We didn't know quite what to expect from her early therapy regimen with Matthew. Realistic expectations, especially in the beginning, are critical. Therapy did not "fix" him; nothing was going to do that. But it did improve the quality of our son's life. It also made us as parents feel we were doing all we could to make his life the best it could be. All of that was more than worth it.

Physical therapy sessions can be difficult and time-consuming. Doing them in your home has advantages, including decreased travel time. But they still invade your space and require adjustments to family schedules. Dads can get impatient with all that. It can even become a point of tension for everyone. Keep focused on the big picture and the benefits it brings to your child.

Working well with therapists calls for the same skill-set we need with other health professionals. Good communication is key. Ask questions. Learn about the exercises/treatments they're using with your child. Discuss the goals behind those treatments. Check in regularly on progress toward those goals. Learn how to do follow-up exercises at home. A caring, educated and involved dad will make a good therapy program even better.

A physical therapist taught me one of the most important lessons I ever learned as the father of a child with disabilities. I was lucky to learn it close to home. Matthew's great-grandfather was Dr. Miland Knapp, a kind, loving, and gentle man, who also happened to be Minnesota's very first doctor of physical medicine. Dr. Knapp was an honored international expert who worked closely with the famed Sister Kenny who revolutionized treatment for polio patients in the 1940s. Today the Miland E. Knapp Rehabilitation Center in Minneapolis carries on his work and legacy.

Grampa Knapp talked to me one day about physical therapy. "Physical exercises won't heal paralyzed muscles," he told me. "Find the muscles that work and make them stronger. We need to look at what a person *can* do, not at what they *can't* do. That's how physical therapy improves quality of life."

Focus on what a person can do, not on what they can't do. Those wise words from Grampa/Dr. Knapp helped me see my children with fresh eyes. It was easy to focus on the "negatives." My son, Matthew, could not *do* much. He would never walk, eat, or speak normally. He would never drive a car, hold a job, or get married. But what could Matthew *do*? He could smile, laugh, and love people. He could enjoy all his "favorites," including raspberry yogurt, Willie Wonka, computer games, reading books, and wrestling with his dad on the living room floor. He overcame countless health crises with a determination that amazed his doctors (not to mention his mom and dad). That is what my son could do.

Dr. Knapp's lesson presented a new way of looking at my sons. It meant focusing on their can-do's, not their can't do's. It taught me to celebrate strengths rather than feel sad, even depressed about weaknesses.

Dad, how are you "seeing" your child these days? See your little boy or girl with fresh eyes. Focus on—celebrate!—what they *can* do. I learned that from a physical therapist, and I hope I never forget it.

Social Workers

*Raising a child with special needs raises lots of questions.
Where will they get medical care? Where will they go to
school? Where will they live? Will they find fulfilling
work? Who will pay for all this? Thank God for social
workers.*

Not far from where I live is Stoney Brook Farms, the site of what they claim is the world's largest corn maze. There are 32 miles of winding pathways spread across 110 acres of Minnesota farmland, and is so big it has its own GPS system. They advise you to bring your phone in case you get lost. Sounds like a good idea.

The world dads like us live in often feels like a maze. From early on you confront a complex and often confusing array of options and decisions surrounding your child's needs. There are choices to be made about medical care, intervention and therapy programs, and before you know it, school systems. Later you face decisions about transition support, assisted employment, and housing. Figuring out the finances of all that raises other questions. Navigating that maze can leave you feeling brain-tired, discouraged, even overwhelmed. That's where social workers come in and why they're so important. Think of them like your personal GPS guiding your through your maze. We'd be lost without them.

We work with social workers in hospitals, schools, county offices, and group homes. What do they do exactly? They find available programs and the funding to pay for them. They make key connections, wrangle paperwork (no fun for anybody), answer your questions, and keep in touch to see how things are going. Next to parents, social workers see the big picture of your child's life better than anybody.

Many social workers bring decades of experience to your child's case. Treasure them. Some are brand-new. Be patient with them. A few might be cold and intimidating; most are friendly and helpful. You'll be glad you have him or her, especially in crisis situations. I met my first social workers during Matthew's initial hospital stay. They introduced me to the alphabet-soup of important programs like SSI, RSDI, MA, WIC, and Tefra. My head—already spinning with new medical challenges and jargon—struggled to keep track of all that. Social workers patiently helped me navigate my maze. They still do. They will for you, too.

Here's one helpful lesson I learned from good social workers: things work out. They really do. Forms get finished, even though at times it feels like you're drowning in them. Finances get figured out and bills get paid. School changes and—later on—housing needs can look like insurmountable mountains. But having survived hundreds of meetings over forty years, signing thousands of forms, and getting over those mountains with the help of good social workers, I can assure you—things do work out.

Another practical tip: let the dust settle. Some days multiple needs, all of them seemingly urgent, scream at you from different directions. (Think whack-a-mole). A form needs to be completed and notarized, a late bill needs to get paid, copies need to be made and mailed, verifications are required. At least a dozen times I've received threatening letters from various agencies telling me that unless "X" happens by "X-date" my son's benefits would end. Scary, but it doesn't happen. My favorite? A Social Security letter informing me Matthew was no longer eligible for benefits because there was no proof he was my son. Oh, brother.

Yes, legitimate, authentically-urgent situations do happen and need our swift attention. Much more often, wheels grind slowly. Items pass in the mail, computer-generated letters are oddly-timed, paperwork gets lost on somebody's desk. If you live in a large city with a big social service system, delays and miscommunications are not unusual. Don't worry about everything. Give it time. Let the dust settle.

Some "social work stress" is unavoidable. Getting medical equipment, such as a new wheelchair, can be a huge hassle. Medical bills + insurance companies + government programs + bureaucracies = a bad mix. Persistence, patience, and a good social worker will get the job done.

Communicate well with your child's social worker. (Over-communicating weakens your standing with them, so avoid that). Honor deadlines. Be positive and respectful. Getting tired, frustrated, or angry at things that happen (or don't happen) with your child, and taking that out on the social worker, doesn't help anyone.

Yes, it can sometimes feel like you're in line at the local DMV holding Claim Check 47. Your social worker should help you when that happens. If they don't have your back, if emails and/or phone calls aren't being returned or communications have broken down, get other people (namely supervisors) involved. Bottom line: get your child the help they need. Nothing is more important.

Fathers play different roles with social workers, depending on family dynamics. Determine who will be Phone Call Maker. Record Keeper. Calendar and Deadline Monitor. Form Signer. Bill Payer. When it comes to paperwork, you'll learn early that organizing records is hugely important and takes more time than you usually think. Don't let those paper piles get too high!

Social workers will also march in and out of your child's parade at a pretty quick pace. I'm very thankful for Emily who's been Andrew's county case manager for nearly a decade. I asked Emily recently how parents—and especially dads—can best handle the "social work" world. With her permission, here's what she told me.

"First, while parents should have hopes and dreams for their children, they also need to be open to changes. Change is a reality of life. Navigating disability services only increases that. When a parent's vision doesn't align with the children's preferences or the current circumstances of their supports or abilities, it's important for parents to be flexible in their goals for their children rather than being discouraged that one exact idea isn't coming to fruition.

"Second, everyone in disability services is busy and your child's needs are important. Both of these are true statements and can sometimes be at odds with each other. Parents who are persistent while still being kind and understanding can build incredibly positive relationships with the people supporting their child.

"Third, parents who advocate for their child with clear, detailed requests have a higher likelihood of receiving positive support rather than pushback from social workers. When parents clearly articulate what they are hoping and looking for—and why—it helps social workers match the need of the child with available services. Then, take feedback from professionals about how that can work within the reality of the services available."

Thank you, Emily! Thanks to all the social workers who patiently guide us and help us find our way.

Hospitals

Our kids will very likely spend time in a hospital. Dads go along for that ride. We soon discover that hospitals can be strange places. Good planning can help all of us survive and even thrive in them.

Many people have an impact on our kids and on us. So do many places. One place many of us get to know well is a hospital. Time in a hospital, short or long term, isn't fun for anyone. Knowing what's coming, and getting ready for it, can help.

Your child might be in the hospital for different reasons. A surgery. A serious illness can get them admitted, too. Maybe they go there for some type of treatment. Sadly, sudden accidents or injuries happen as well. Whatever the reason, however long the stay, hospital life presents challenges. We'd all rather be home.

Hospitals are a paradox. They're stressful—yet boring. They're cold and sterile—but often connect us with warm and supportive people. We hate hospitals—but we love that they're available for our kids when we need them. Hospitals are reception desks, waiting rooms, long hallways, elevators, cafeterias, ERs, surgical wards, parking ramps, public bathrooms, consult rooms, nursing desks, and lobbies, filled with people of all ages, shapes, sizes and colors, and medical needs. No two hospitals are alike, yet they can all feel the same.

I've gotten to know hospitals too well. First there was Hahneman, then Memorial, soon followed by the University of Massachusetts Medical Center in Worcester. Later, Boston Children's Hospital, the "Floating Hospital" at Tufts University, and Boston General. In Minnesota we went to the University of Minnesota Hospital, Minneapolis Children's, Abbott-Northwestern, Maple Grove Hospital, Methodist Hospital, Buffalo Hospital, St. Paul United, Unity Hospital in Fridley, the Mayo Clinic in Rochester, Abbott-Northwestern, Gillette Children's in St. Paul, and North Memorial. In California we went to Los Gatos Hospital, Lucile Salter Packard Children's Hospital at Stanford, and Good Samaritan. Whew.

I'm thankful for all the hospitals we've experienced. Both my sons received medical care in those places that saved their lives more than once. Hospitals create war stories, though; I hope you haven't had too many. Over time bad memories evaporate, good memories linger. That helps.

I received an extended introduction into hospital life with Matthew's nearly year-long stay in intensive care. It felt like living in a war zone. Life-and-death scenarios played out all around us 24/7, with children—very sick and seriously injured—lying in curtained cubicles circling a large room. Buzzers and alarms were the soundtrack of that place. (Premature babies whose alarms seemingly rang non-stop were affectionately called "dingers.") Doctors and nurses buzzed from bed-to-bed like bees tending hives. The young patients, usually not conscious, were eerily quiet. Thankfully, most of those kids made it. Sadly, some did not.

Our long stay in ICU was unusual. Whatever your hospital stays are like with your child, know that with grit and patience you can and will get through them. Keep your eyes (and hearts) open to encounter a few heroes along the way—we'll never forget you, Little Paul!—and even an unexpected smile or two. Here are five practical strategies to help you make the best of hospital life.

First, accept hospitals for what they are—a place for sick people. That explains their overall serious, even somber atmosphere. Children's hospitals often try to create a friendlier, homier feel, and that helps. Be thankful for any warm, human touches your hospital may provide. Don't expect them, though. A hospital is a place no one wants to be.

Second, hospitals are busy people doing difficult jobs. Doctors, nurses, therapists, administrators, and support staff put in long hours on jobs most people would never want to do. Crisis is routine. Many hospital employees view their work as a calling and are inspiring to be around. It's disheartening but also true that others approach what they do as just a job to pay the bills. Lots of people-stuff swirls around you in a hospital— the good, the bad, the ugly. You see and deal with a lot.

Third, the longer your stay, the harder it gets. Hospitals aren't hotels. We are there with our kids. Caring for us isn't their priority and shouldn't be. Be thankful for any efforts extended your way. To survive (never mind thrive) in a hospital after more than a few days you need to take care of yourself. Get enough sleep somehow. Plan your meals. (Avoid vending machines, if possible). Find a place to grab a shower. Bring fresh clothes. Have stuff with you (books, an iPad, headphones, snacks) for those inevitable long waits. An hour in a hospital is kind of like dog-years, stretching out for what feels like way more than sixty minutes.

Fourth, enjoy any surprises. A hospital is filled with busy people. Many are also caring and are there for all the right reasons. Appreciate doctors, nurses, and therapists, of course, but others, too, like office staff, receptionists, volunteers, social workers, and cleaning people. My son, Andrew, was hospitalized twice recently for week-long stays. We met excellent doctors and nurses, but other people provided highlights. A therapist showed up one morning with her guitar to fill Andrew's room with fun music. A friendly chaplain dropped by daily, never failing to ask me a simple question: "How are *you* doing?" A smiling volunteer took my spot to help my son eat dinner. Welcome surprising gifts that come your way.

Fifth, cozy up your child's room. A hospital can be cold and sterile, especially for kids. For longer stays, bring in a familiar picture or two. Favorite books help. So does music. Don't let blaring TVs (seemingly *everywhere* in hospitals these days) set the tone. If allowed, bring in snacks for your child to munch on. A note of caution about personal items (and safety): hospitals are big public places. Keep an eye on valuables, purses, toys, books, etc. Things can happen.

Each hospital stay becomes a unique a story of its own. With prior planning, dads can make that story better for everyone. Then, hopefully, after a happy ending, we all get to head home.

10
School

When your child reaches school-age, big changes affect everyone. The flow of the school calendar, and dealing with teachers, homework, and meetings, can be consuming. Be part of that and enjoy what you can—it passes very quickly!

A hospital is one place your child may get to know well. A more positive, fun, and life-changing place will be his or her school. A child with special needs entering the world of school faces all kinds of challenges. So does his or her dad.

Let's be thankful our kids experience school now. Not all that long ago a child with disabilities was not welcome in public schools. They did not "fit" there and were shuffled off to "special" classes in "special" rooms with "special" teachers. Times have changed. 21st-century schools are better equipped to meet the needs of students with disabilities. While nothing is perfect, it is certainly better.

More than seven million American school children (about 14% of all students ages 3-21) are eligible for special education services. A key turning point in our country was passing the Individuals with Disabilities Education Act (IDEA) in 1990, key legislation that required children with disabilities to be provided "free appropriate public education in the least restrictive environment." Challenges remain but IDEA is the law and makes a difference for kids like ours. We can and should be thankful for that.

What should that look like in your child's school? Your son or daughter is legally required to receive educational support appropriate to their needs. Practically speaking for parents like us, it also means lots of meetings, discussions, phone calls, paperwork, advocacy, hard work, patience, flexibility, a few bumps along the way, and no doubt a few headaches. All of that is needed to help our son or daughter reach their potential in the school environment. Dads are needed every step of the way.

Your child has disabilities and unique needs. Their diagnosis—and how the school will serve their needs—is documented in their Individualized Educational Plan (IEP). Think of it as the "bible" of your child's school experience. An IEP gets up-dated yearly and keeps everyone—teachers, administrators, para-professionals, and parents—on the same page. Read it. Know it well. It's key to your child's success in school.

My sons have had great schools with some extraordinary teachers. (The few who weren't made the "stars" shine even brighter). You'll encounter teachers and administrators who authentically care about kids with special needs. You will remember those people the rest of your life.

I met many at Juana Briones School in Palo Alto, California, where Matthew attended elementary school. Briones was a diverse school mixing able-bodied and disabled kids. From the minute you walked on campus, you knew something was different. K-6 classrooms were in two connected wings forming a big "L" with a large, shared playground between them. All students moved in-and-out of those classrooms throughout the day, creating a delightful mix of integrated activities and spontaneous, informal interactions.

You've never seen so many wheelchairs, braces, lifts and pieces of adapted equipment in your life! What you *really* saw were just kids—all shapes, sizes, colors, and ability levels doing school, and sharing life, together. Everybody was included in everything. You saw kids learning, laughing, playing, eating lunch together, going on field trips, waiting for rides at day's end. One sweet memory: watching Matthew casually getting tube-fed while his classmate-buddy sat next to him munching on his peanut-butter sandwich. Somehow it all just worked.

That started with a commitment by the faculty that "mainstreaming" would be more than a word. Were their challenges? Of course, but they were overcome with a can-do spirit, creativity, flexibility, patience, hard work, and humor. I'm so thankful for teachers like Marshall C. (Mr. Rogers' twin separated at birth?), Paul A. (never without a beaming smile and colorful beret), Polly M. (every classroom's firm but loving "mom"), and many others. Teachers like that are worth a hundred good IEPs.

I hope you find great schools and teachers for your child. It doesn't just happen. It takes on-line research, phone calls, site visits, and lots of discussion. It also means being aware of the challenges schools face today. Nearly 80 percent of schools struggle to hire qualified staff to provide those services, according to the Department of Education. Prior to Juana Briones, Matthew attended a rural elementary school with good staff but was so overwhelmed with his needs they advised us to seek alternative placement. Helping find what's best for our kids means looking at the situation from everyone's perspective.

School life for and with our kids isn't easy. Here are some practical suggestions as you face these critical years.

Get ready for lots of meetings. Developing an appropriate and workable IEP for your child is hard work and takes time. Extra time isn't always something dads like us have. But make school a priority.

Commit to be involved. Dad, your child's school success does not rest all on your shoulders, but your shoulders need to be in those school meetings and on those phone calls. Many times people assume mom will handle all "school stuff." That isn't good for anyone, your child, their mom, or you. Be a partner. Get involved. Advocate for your child at school Remember, we only get one shot at this.

Use resources your child's school can (and is legally required to) provide. Your child will qualify for special modifications, classroom assistance, testing adaptations, and more. Do your homework, find out what those resources provide, and use them! It's the law. It's also the right thing to do.

One resource that became a huge highlight in Andrew's school life was the adapted sports program at his junior and senior high schools. Andrew loved sports, especially basketball. (In third grade he told me he planned to play in the NBA someday. "That's great, Andrew," I told him, "but when we watch games on TV do we see any players in a wheelchair?" He thought for a moment, gave me a confident smile, and said, "I'll be the first!") Obviously my son couldn't compete with able-bodied kids. But the adapted sports program—run by dedicated coaches and volunteers—offered basketball, floor hockey, softball, bowling and more. Quality was always top-notch—good equipment, uniforms, referees, tournaments, trophies, season-ending banquets, everything. All of that boosted my son's confidence and self-esteem and made those years some of the best of his life.

Find what works for your child and help them go for it! It might be adapted sports. It might be music, theater, dance, art, writing, who knows? Those school-time "extras" are an investment in your child's life that make a difference.

Communicate regularly with teachers. Talk in person, send needed emails, make phone calls, attend conferences. When possible, volunteer for book fairs, sporting events, carnivals, fundraisers, as a tutor or lunchroom monitor. Stay connected!

Your child's school years are hugely important. While nothing is perfect (that word doesn't exist in our world, does it), good teachers, caring administrators, consistent communication, and your involvement will make those years the best they can be. For everyone.

11

Loneliness

Dads like us often feel isolated. Knowing that every person feels that at times does help. So does reaching out to connect with other people. Finding and leaning on a good friend or two is huge. So is being willing to take a risk!

There are times when we feel different from "normal" dads. When that happens to me, I try to remember Dumbo the Elephant.

You remember him, the star of that Disney movie. Dumbo had really big ears. They were so big he felt "different" from the other elephants. He didn't fit into normal circus life, leaving him isolated and lonely. Except for one friend, no one quite knew what to do with Dumbo.

The good news is that Dumbo eventually overcomes that by using his big ears to do something pretty special. In his case, he took risks and learned how to fly. Everyone in the circus ended up accepting and even admiring Dumbo, giving a nice, happily-ever-after ending to his story.

Feeling "different" is part of our story, too, starting early with our kids. I remember picking Andrew up from elementary school one day. All the other kids were on the playground, laughing, running, kicking a soccer ball. I found Andrew sitting alone on a swing. He didn't fit in. It was hard for him.

It was hard for his dad, too. Our hearts ache when we see our kids isolated because of their disabilities. We feel some of that ourselves as we awkwardly rub shoulders with dads whose kids are moving on in life, excelling in school, sports, the arts, relationships, everything it seems. We want everything to be normal for our kids, too—but it isn't. And it won't be.

What can we do when being different isolates our children—and us?

Face the painful realities. Our children *are* different. Dads like us are different. Life isn't what we expected it to be. However that happened for our son or daughter—bad genetic wiring, mish-mashed chromosomes, a serious illness, a horrible accident—our son or daughter is disabled. Our kid is different, our family is different, dads like us are different. That's painful to acknowledge, but it's where we need to start.

Realize we often self-inflict and exaggerate those feelings. Our "differentness" is very noticeable at times. Pushing a kid in a wheelchair through a crowd gets noticed. A child with obvious physical deformities gets stared at. Trying to calm your son or daughter's emotional autistic-based breakdown in a crowded mall is hard for people to ignore. Difficult moments can be isolating.

But we aren't the only people (or dads) who feel those things. Everyone feels lonely and isolated at times. It's part of being human. It helps to remember that. It also helps to know that what's happening with our child (in that crowd, at that mall, wherever) might be a bigger deal to us than it really is. We get more sensitive to this stuff than we need to be. There's nothing to see here, people, just move on. Dad, you can move on, too.

Overcome isolation by connecting with others. Talking about our child can help. It can also be tough. Barriers exist, from both directions. People may shy away from wanting to pry into your life. Most people also agree it's harder for men to talk about it than women. But we can do it. Screw up the courage. Look for good listeners. Tell your stories. Celebrate your kid. He or she is worth celebrating!

Dumbo found an unlikely friend in Timothy Q. Mouse and it changed his life. We should stay open to a few surprises, too. One late night I sat in another waiting room after another surgery. Suddenly Terry walked in, a quiet, stocky guy with a big red beard who looked more like a lumberjack than the auto mechanic he was. We'd met at church but didn't know each other well. We shook hands, said hello, and for the next hour pretty much sat there in silence. Strange? A little. Helpful? Totally. Just by being there, Terry helped me feel less isolated and less alone. Here's a kicker. I never saw Terry again in my life. Ever. But his unexpected, but timely gift of friendship that one evening is a gift I still value. Welcome the Terrys in your life.

Learn to fly! With Timothy's encouragement, Dumbo learned his big ears could actually help him fly. The thing that had made him feel "different" actually became his strength. Pretty ironic and very cool. How can dads like us learn to fly? By accepting that our world is "different" but choosing to rise above it. That isn't easy, either, and it means taking some risks.

Matthew at age five was still dealing with multiple medical challenges, including daily apnea spells. When friends (whose sweet little daughter about Matthew's age also had spina bifida) invited us to vacation with them in the Virgin Islands at a donated condo, it sounded too good to be true. And impossible to pull off. The complications of a trip seemed mind-boggling. Airports? Plane rides? Two wheelchairs? An oxygen concentrator? What happens if either (both?) of the kids get sick, needs a doctor, never mind a hospital? In a foreign country? Thanks, but no thanks. Too risky.

I told them, they understood, but I immediately felt angry. Angry about missing a trip I knew we'd love. Angry because I felt denied what "normal" people would do. I reconsidered. I took a risk and decided to go for it! It all worked out. Today I have priceless memories of Matthew casually sitting on a catamaran soaking up the Caribbean sunshine with a huge smile on his face. We were all flying!

Most of the "flying" dads like us do won't be like that. We fly in ordinary, simple ways. We fly by living full and active lives in the face of family challenges. We fly when we choose to be good dads, love our kids and families, work hard at our jobs, and make the best of each day. Sure, we still feel a little different and isolated at times. We face that by courageously connecting with others and by taking a few risks. Thanks, Dumbo. See you in the clouds.

Career

Your career is a big part of your life. Keep it in healthy balance. Talk to your boss (and colleagues) as needed about your family situation. Use job-related supports. Don't expect too much—or too little—of yourself on the job.

It had been a rough day. Matthew's five-hour surgery that morning to reposition bones in his feet had gone well but he was in lots of pain. I stayed with him all day and through the night, grabbing fitful sleep in the recliner next to his bed. The next morning in a closet-sized public bathroom I changed into my suit and tie. (Note to self: paper towels are lousy for shining shoes). I had to look nice, though. As a pastor in a local church, I was on my way to officiate a wedding.

You and I are fathers of kids with disabilities and special needs. But we're more than that. We're husbands and partners, dads of other children perhaps, brothers, friends. We're also men who have jobs. There are bills to pay and careers to build. Our professions are important to us. We cannot and should not ignore that key part of our lives.

Jobs are a two-sided coin for us. One side is positive. Work is good. It fulfills us. Work gives us a place to be creative in tasks we (hopefully) enjoy with people we (usually) like. A job can also provide healthy "escape" from stress we face with our child's challenges. "Pouring yourself into your job to deal with outside pressures isn't always a bad thing," my supervisor once told me. I think she's right.

There's a negative side to that coin, too. Our job often feels like a huge burden. Coordinating work projects and deadlines, business travel, email traffic, and committee meetings, with medical appointments, school conferences, therapy sessions, and surgeries (never mind a few unscheduled trips to the ER) feels like you're trying—and usually failing—to juggle five balls at once.

Times are changing. When it comes to job and family responsibilities, the 21st century work culture is increasingly supportive of working parents, and dads in particular. Paternity leave is more commonplace. Even with those changes, tensions may still exist. Being called away for child-related needs doesn't always go over well at your workplace. Maybe your boss doesn't care about what you're going through with your child. Some co-workers might feel the same.

Sometimes those pressures are self-inflicted. We strive hard to be a good employee AND a good dad. Somedays maybe too hard. We worry that our struggle to juggle family and job needs might lead others to see us as vulnerable (or even expendable). We try to hide that from others. We keep our head down and plow ahead as if everything is just fine—even when we know it isn't.

How are you balancing being a dad like us with being a good employee? Here are practical tips to help you face that ongoing challenge.

Say yes to your job. What you do is important, for many reasons. Don't ignore or downplay it. That's not fair to you or to the people for whom you work. Give it your best.

Know it won't be easy. The dad who thinks the stress of raising a child with special needs won't affect his work performance is kidding himself. Trying to totally separate or compartmentalize our work and parenting lives isn't sustainable. Admitting that is a wise place to start.

Keep communicating! Your boss, and to some extent your co-workers, need to be aware of your situation. Not all the details, of course, but enough information to help them realize you might be called away for child-related meetings and medical appointments. Don't worry about vulnerability. Be a professional. Tell people what they need to know when they need to know it. That will help you and them.

Find and use available supports. Important laws and regulations are in place to help our kids—and us. The Family Medical Leave Act (FMLA) is one of the most important, guaranteeing job protection if/when we need to be away from work for extended periods of time. Getting it in place requires forms and "doctor's notes," but it's worth it. Your Human Resource department should assist you with it, even if you never need to use it. It's definitely a stress-reliever.

Lean on smart people. Sharing your family situation with people at work—appropriately, of course—can connect you with valuable resources. When I told a co-worker that having two kids in wheelchairs made for transportation challenges, she told me about grants available through our employee assistance fund, and even helped with the paperwork! Within weeks I received help to purchase an accessible van. For the first time post-wheelchairs our family was able to travel somewhere together. What a gift!

Find a good mentor, or two. A mentor can help you navigate the unique balance of work and parenting a child with special needs. Finding a mentor with his own "dads like us" story hits the jackpot. The main thing: find someone you respect who can be a listening ear, sounding board, wise guide, and friend.

Have realistic expectations. There will be times at work when you aren't functioning at 100 percent. You might feel like a failure; you aren't. Life—and work—is an up-and-down experience for everybody. We all have right foot/left foot days. Don't expect too much of yourself. Or too little, either.

Before Matthew turned two, he was back in the hospital and not doing well. At the same time I was offered a new job. It meant a promotion and I wanted to take it. The problem? It was in a town 50 miles away. Doctors weren't promising a quick recovery for our son, which made my decision all the more difficult. One of the doctors knew I was struggling and shared some advice in a letter. His main message: "Don't allow your child's disabilities or health needs to totally control your life." I understood his point, but I still struggled with competing priorities. I ended up taking the job. Matthew returned home in a relatively short time. Things worked out. Life has a way of working out.

That wasn't the last time work-life balance would challenge me. You've faced your own challenges—or will—in in days ahead. It's just a big part of being a dad like us. It isn't easy. We struggle. We may second-guess ourselves at time. But we move ahead, doing all we can to be the best dad and employee we can be.

13

Self-Care

All fathers get stressed. Dads of children who are disabled and have special needs get some extra portions. We handle stress best by taking care of ourselves. That's a decision we have to make every day. So...just do it!

All parents get stressed. There's no end to daily chores: get the kids to school on time, prep for that meeting with the boss, pay the bills, mow the lawn, fix the car. Every household has pressures. Parents of kids who are disabled experience all that "normal" stress—and a bit more.

Stress takes a toll on our physical and mental health. Unrelieved stress can even shorten your life, especially in long-term care situations. (40 percent of people caring for loved ones with Alzheimer's die before the patient does.). Stress can also harm relationships. It diminishes job performance. It can lead to destructive behaviors and addictions. All serious stuff.

How do we best handle stress? It comes down to decisions—one, two, maybe a dozen each day—to take care of ourselves. To make our own personal health number one. That sounds selfish; it really isn't. You've heard the cliches. "You can't take care of other people if you don't take care of yourself first." "Fill yourself up so you'll have something to give others." And from that friendly flight attendant: "Put on your own oxygen mask before helping anyone else, even your child." That advice may get tiresome, but it's true. Self-care needs to be priority one, especially for dads like us.

I've known different kinds of stress in caring for my sons. One I call microwave stress. That's when something traumatic suddenly and unexpectedly happens—a serious fall, a high fever, an emergency surgery. You can't plan for it. It just quickly happens.

Matthew has a small mechanical pump in his brain called a shunt that drains spinal fluid. It works very well—most of the time. When shunts fail, things happen. One pleasant summer afternoon in the middle of a family photo shoot, my six-year-old was happy and smiling. Seconds later he was slumped over in his wheelchair, unconscious. We called 911 and within two hours he was in surgery to replace his clogged shunt. That evening he was happy and smiling again. That's microwave stress.

Then there's "crockpot stress," the constant, low-simmering pressure fueled by long-term, on-going worries and anxieties that are part of raising a child with disabilities. We feel stress about long-term medical needs, school issues, financial pressures, their future, and more. We may not be aware of crockpot-stress every day, but it's there and it wears us down.

Taking care of ourselves helps us manage stress. Why'd don't we do that better? We get busy. Days fill up with family and work responsibilities. A sudden illness or unexpected surgery can disrupt routines for weeks at a time. Taking care of ourselves doesn't seem like a priority. So we ignore it. I'll think about that tomorrow, we say.

What does good self-care look like? It really is a matter of making simple choices.

Exercise regularly. Be physically active, every day. Plan regular workouts. 3-5 times a week is best, fitness experts say. Take a daily walk, jog, bike, lift weights, play tennis, whatever works for you and that you enjoy. Exercise releases natural tranquilizers, so take advantage of that free medicine!

This is a daily battle for everyone. Don't be too hard on yourself when you struggle and feel like you're failing. A fitness trainer once told me three consecutive days of workouts pretty much guarantees a refreshed life. That sounds do-able and is worth a try!

Eat healthy. When I get stressed, I want to eat. Not fruit and vegetables, of course, but cookies, candy, the more chocolate the better. Does this sound familiar? You're at the hospital with your child for tests, a doctor or clinic visit, treatments, whatever. You sit and wait. A candy machine in the lobby is staring at you. Been there, eaten that. "I need/deserve something," you think. A sugar rush feels good but leaves you unsatisfied and wanting more. Healthy eating is a daily battle we need to fight and win, a huge part of taking care of ourselves and handling stress.

Get enough sleep. Stress disrupts sleep. Sleep deprivation is common for dads like us. Sleep-deprived people make bad decisions. They also make bad husbands, partners, and fathers. How much sleep do you need to function best? Get that amount, somehow. Maybe power naps are your thing. Again, whatever works for you.

Keep your medical appointments. You wouldn't think of ignoring your child's medical calendar. How are you with your own? That can be easy to overlook, and even easier to rationalize when you do. Get your scheduled physicals, have your eyes checked, see the dentist. You might be sick of seeing doctors; not seeing them will make you sicker. You need to monitor your health, for your sake, and everyone else's.

Consider your spiritual needs. Whatever that looks like for you, do it.

Make time to play. Do the activities that relax you, charge your batteries, and give your mind (body and spirit, too) a break from stress. How do you like to play? Golf offers a nice break for me, if I don't take it too seriously. So is a long walk or time with a good book. When I don't play, stress builds. How are you "playing" these days?

We handle stress by making self-care a daily priority. That's the smart decision, every time.

Marriage

*Every marriage faces challenges. Parents raising children
with disabilities know unique relationship pressures.
Some days it can all feel impossible. Nothing is more
important than keeping your marriage top priority—
from day one.*

Dads like us don't walk our path alone, of course. Our wife or partner, the mother of our child who is disabled, is on this journey, too. This book is for dads, and we can't begin to touch on all that those often-incredible women face being a "mom like us." We won't even try. The role she plays in the life of the child we share has impact beyond words.

Every child with disabilities is unique. So is every marriage. Only you and your wife know what you have gone through—and are going through—together. No one should presume to tell you they have all the answers to your marriage questions.

One thing we can all agree on is how important our marriage-relationship is to our child. They say the best gift parents can give their kids is a mom and dad who share a loving and peaceful relationship. Given their special needs, that must be even more true for our kids.

Marriage isn't easy for dads like us—or our partners. Raising a physically, mentally, perhaps emotionally, challenged child to survive and thrive in the "normal" world will test you both. It will also test your marriage. "We're going to get out of this thing alive, even if it kills us," my wife, Pam, would often say. Some days that's exactly how it felt.

We rode an emotional roller-coaster while caring for our boys. Some days Pam was cheerful and optimistic while I was feeling drained and discouraged. Then for some reason we'd switch. Steve up, Pam down. We didn't plan that, it just seemed to happen. Have you sensed a similar ride with your partner?

When Matthew was born severely disabled, it was obvious (more to others than ourselves) that we were up against immense pressures as individuals and as a couple. Matthew's first year—lived in a hospital's intensive care unit —was our fourth year of marriage. We were thousands of miles away from home. I was beginning my first full-time job. Trying to handle all that, while building a healthy, happy marriage, wasn't easy. Far from it.

Early on I saw an oft-quoted statistic: "Couples with a disabled child have a divorce rate of 80 percent." Compared to a "normal" divorce rate of 50 percent, that was disturbing. (Newer studies indicate the 80 percent number was probably exaggerated). The numbers didn't matter but they did open my eyes to realities I wanted to ignore.

We lived a bizarre mix of the "routine" (grocery shopping, cutting the lawn, doing laundry) and the "bizarre" (surgeries, physical therapy, tube feedings, daily apnea spells, and CPR). I remember asking the manager at a restaurant for a quiet spot where Pam could use our then suitcase-sized breast pump. "We don't really want to get involved in something like that," he told me. Our family calendar—filled with doctor, school and therapy appointments—looked like a Jackson Pollock painting. We had worries, rarely voiced: "is our little boy going to make it?" A darker, never-spoken question began to lurk as well: "Is our marriage going to make it?"

Sadly, ours did not. Thirty years into our marriage our long road of caregiving for our kids, complicated by Pam's own health struggles (she was diagnosed with Parkinson's disease in 2000 and passed away in 2012), and severely wounded by my personal struggles and failures, ended in divorce. We continued to love and cherish our boys together but our marriage did not survive.

If I could time-travel back to the day before my first son was born, what marriage advice would I give myself? What would I say to any young dad—and husband—like us? Five things, at least.

First, face reality. To borrow Bette Davis' famous movie line, "Fasten your seat-belt, it's going to be a bumpy night." Many of them, actually, and days, too. Being the dad of a child with disabilities will change and challenge every part of your life, including your marriage. It carries the potential to damage and even end your marriage. Scary words. That's not true because you are weak, selfish or bad people. It's true because that's reality. Face it, accept it, and do all you can to deal with it.

Second, keep your marriage top priority. Always. That won't be easy. A hundred things—stressors in all shapes, sizes and intensities—will come screaming at you. Making a commitment to keep your marriage above all of that will be the daily, on-going challenge.

Third, work at the little things. Keep talking. Have regular date nights and frequent get-aways. (Those can be difficult to coordinate; find a workable respite support plan). Celebrate special days, birthdays, and anniversaries. Give gifts. Give hugs. Play together. Don't lose track of each other with everything else going on. That can happen so gradually you'll hardly notice. Carve out regular check-in times to talk about your child, of course, but also to talk about something other than disabilities, doctors and special needs. You both need that.

Fourth, equally share "mental labor." A household runs on physical tasks, like laundry, grocery shopping and meal prep, bill-paying, yard work, kid taxi service, the whole list. Doing those chores is essential; so is the "mental labor," anticipating, planning and monitoring their completion. Studies show wives/moms handle a disproportionate load of mental labor in most families, often leading to frayed relationships. Families of children with disabilities face extra levels of physical and mental labor, making the wise division of work even more imperative.

Fifth, get counselling, early and often. When I think back to our early years of marriage, all that Pam and I experienced and the stress we faced, and realize that we tried doing that without regular mental health support, I am surprised and embarrassed. Simply put, that was stupid. Don't be stupid. You're dealing with tough stuff. Talk about it regularly with a professional counselor. You'll be glad you did. Your marriage will be stronger and better equipped for the long haul.

Sixth, lean on others. Raising kids takes a village, they famously say. Families with a child who is disabled need a big village. Yours can be made up of family members, friends, neighbors, and anyone else who cares about you. Ask for help. Does it feel like you're imposing? Do it anyway. (Paybacks can come later). You need practical, daily support with food, transportation, errands, and help with your other kids, especially during any health crises. Welcome any help that comes. Be thankful for it. Your child needs it, you need it, your wife/partner needs it. Your marriage needs it, too.

This is very painful stuff for me to write. My marriage did not make it. You know your story. You know how your marriage has worked, is working, how you hope it will work in the future. Perhaps you, too, have already faced, or will face, the reality of divorce. That is not what we expected or wanted. But we know that life goes on. We have to travel the road before us, with all of its twists, wherever it leads.

Many couples who have raised a child with disabilities say their marriage actually became better and stronger through that experience. Through awareness, commitment, and hard work—seasoned daily with compassion, forgiveness, and more than a few hugs—may that be your wonderful story, too.

Family Ties

Extended family members can play a key role in your child's life. Know that their early emotions (and struggles) concerning your child might mirror your own to a degree. Communicate regularly with them. Welcome their support.

Each family tree looks different. Your child may have brothers or sisters (presently or in the future), grandparents, great-grandparents, aunts, uncles, and cousins. Your relatives might live close by, far away, or somewhere in between. Maybe you consider yours a "close" family, maybe not. Whatever your family make-up and dynamics, these are people who can, will, and should be an important part of your child's life.

When your child's disability is confirmed—at whatever age—be aware that other people are affected by that news as well. That starts with your relatives. Many will share feelings similar to your own, such as shock, sadness and grief. Not to the same depth as you, of course, but their feelings are just as real and need to be respected. They fostered hopes and dreams about their new brother or sister, grandson, granddaughter, niece, nephew, or cousin. It is easy for us dads—bowled over in our own emotional avalanche—to overlook this.

Each family is unique. None of this is automatic. But what you all go through might bring people closer together. Keeping everyone informed is a big part in how well that will go. Relatives want to hear about diagnoses and prognoses, surgical plans, visitation protocols, and so on. Your relatives love and care for your child. They also love and care for you, your wife or partner, and for any siblings in the mix.

It can be challenging to keep everybody adequately informed, especially during times of medical stress. Communication is also hard when family members live far away. When Matthew was born in

Massachusetts, Pam's family was in Minnesota, and my closest relatives were scattered across California, Utah, Montana, and Alaska. Phone calls can be hard. Today's technology, including Facetime, Zoom, and caringbridge.org, makes that easier. It all starts, though, with a commitment to keep family members in the loop, even when that's tough to do.

Who needs timely updates? Your other children, of course. What's happening with their new little sister or brother affects them more than anyone else, outside of mom and dad. They've been eagerly anticipating this special family-moment for months. Give them as much one-on-one time as you can, answer their questions, offer needed assurances. Even in the hard stuff, do all you can to help everyone celebrate the precious new life who has joined your family.

Priceless bonds often develop between siblings, even more so when one of them has disabilities and special needs. Big brother or sister can become your child's lifelong best friend, guide, teacher, protector, and helper. Be sensitive to potential difficulties, too. When huge amounts of time and attention are given to one child's care, other siblings may feel neglected. Wise parents sense if this is happening and do what they can to make sure no one feels left out.

Grandparents may have the most complex family tie with your child. They've looked forward to this new child—and this new phase of their own lives—with joyous anticipation. When they learn there's "something wrong" with the baby or child, they might be devastated. They might even go through their own season of denial. Grandparents will worry about your child's health and future. As your parents, they're also worrying about you.

How can dads help grandparents? Be sensitive to their feelings. Be realistic about the support they can offer while needing some of their own. Keep them informed of your child's (their grandchild's) medical situation. Find resources to help them understand what the future may hold. (There are scores of helpful articles, podcasts, and videos on the internet.) Don't hesitate to lean on their parental experience, wisdom, and objectivity, as needed. They've been down the parenting road before, even if the circumstances are different.

Your family tree also has aunts, uncles and cousins. Hopefully they'll provide wonderful love and smiles, too. Accept their offers to help. Close and caring relatives might be some of your first and best "listening ears."

Every family tree has curved branches, some more curved than others. Many families of children with disabilities have "step" relatives: step-parents, brothers, sisters, and grandparents. I secretly wish one of those Brady kids had been in a wheelchair to show us what a "perfect" blended family might look like! That didn't happen so we'll have to figure it out on our own. With patience and love, over time, we will.

Here's a brief but deserved shout-out to step-parents. It's been said the only job tougher than being a parent is being a step-parent. Consider the women who welcome a child with special needs into their lives through a relationship with the father. It is not easy. A trained therapist may be especially helpful to families making that choice. Hopefully, we all do the best we can, loving each other and seeking the good of the child.

Treasure your family tree! Every person in it has the potential to be a special gift to your child. May the shade of that tree be a place where our kids find love, acceptance and support, all the things they need most.

16

Advocate

Your child needs advocates—people who know them well, understand their needs, and stand up for them. We might shy away from doing that because it can include tension and conflict. But dads like us need to be good advocates.

"Advocate" is a legal term that means a lawyer or counselor. An advocate speaks up for someone else when for whatever reason that person isn't able speak up for himself or herself. Think of it as a hat we need to be willing to wear for our kids.

Advocacy takes many forms, but basically it's when you speak up for your child. It is you making sure their needs are met. Sometimes that can seem trivial. ("Please let the staff know that my son likes to watch *The Price is Right* every morning at 10.") Some are big. ("Is major brain surgery the only option?"). Our children face unique challenges. When they can't speak up for themselves, someone needs to. Why wouldn't that be us?

We wear our advocate hat in meetings with doctors, teachers, therapists, and social workers. With real-world people, too, like landlords, the cable guy, a shoe salesman in a mall, crowds of people on a busy street. ("Excuse us, please, wheelchair here"). You might even need to advocate for your child with family members and friends. You wear that hat with care teams, transition programs, churches, job sites, group homes, in your neighborhood. Maybe even on a playground or two.

Here are some examples of times I needed to advocate for my sons:

• One doctor recommended surgery; a second was against it. I asked questions and did my best to understand the differing opinions. A good decision was ultimately reached.

• In a new hospital Matthew was given medication that resulted in awful side effects. I noticed it, spoke up, and meds were changed. What would have happened if I kept quiet?

• A certain nurse was cold, borderline harsh, in her bedside cares. I had a difficult conversation with the nurse case manager but the situation was rectified.

• Andrew's day program proposed a schedule change that would significantly alter his daily routine. I knew change was difficult for him. (That's true for many of our kids). I respectfully asked them to explore other options. A compromise was reached.

• Matthew was placed on hospice care at one point in his mid-30s and given only weeks to live. After sensing his condition was stronger than what the hospice team originally determined, I directed them to remove him from hospice and resume feedings. Within days his health stabilized.

You'd think that advocating for our kids would be an easy, natural fit for us. We love our child. We know and love him or her dearly. We certainly want the best for them. Some dads are naturals and get energized by wearing the advocate's hat. Some moms are "mama bears." I guess there are "papa bears," too. Maybe that describes you.

But being an advocate isn't always easy. It means staying informed about complex issues. It means holding people accountable. Sometimes we feel overmatched, especially with doctors. Another barrier? We don't want to get into an adversarial relationship with the people who are taking care of our child. Sometimes we just get tired, worn down by too many battles. We get tempted to back off and let somebody else figure it all out.

Two incidents, horribly similar, challenged me to be a good advocate. In the first I failed miserably. The second went much better.

Incident One: On a group home outing Matthew's wheelchair tumbled down a small flight of stairs. He fell forward, broke his nose, chipped a tooth, and cracked a small bone in his chin. His injuries, bad enough, could have been worse. The staff invited me to a meeting to review their incident report. It was a chance for me to ask hard questions. What happened exactly? Why did it happen? Who failed to supervise him? How do we make sure nothing like this ever happens again? I had all kinds of necessary questions in my head.

One staff member spoke up. "Matthew pushed himself down those steps. We feel bad. It won't happen again." My son, a paralyzed, vision-impaired, vulnerable adult, is 100% dependent on others for his safety. Blaming him was unacceptable if not legally liable. Matthew needed a strong advocate at that moment. It needed to be me.

Instead, I just sat there, listening to their apology. They seemed sincere. I felt bad for Matthew. I felt bad for them. This was Matthew's first group home. Mine, too. I was relieved he hadn't suffered major injuries and wanted to pretend the whole thing never happened. I'm still ashamed of my weak performance in that meeting. My advocate hat was sitting right there. I failed to put it on.

Incident Two: Three years later Matthew is in a new group home. I get a phone call. "Your son was being transferred in the bathroom when a strap on the lift broke. He fell and hit his head on the floor. We called for an ambulance." I rush to (yet) another ER, a firestorm of fear and anger raging in my head. Not again! A developmentally-disabled person, with a shunt in his brain, no less, doesn't need another fall on his head! How in the hell could this have happened?!

Matthew was conscious and even smiled at me when I entered his room. His face was swollen, he had a big black eye and a large, freshly-stitched cut on his forehead. Thankfully, X-rays confirmed no skull fracture, brain swelling, or shunt damage. My tough little fighter was going to be okay—again.

This time I felt and acted very different. I told the staff to schedule a meeting the next day with their supervisor. At that meeting I learned that the attendant who had been with Matthew during the fall wouldn't attend. "He is suspended," the supervisor said. "We need to get questions answered." Yes, we certainly do, and I immediately started asking them.

What exactly happened? How did Matthew fall? How far did he fall? What did they do immediately after he fell? I ask to see the broken strap. They bring me a thick piece of canvas about two feet in length, now in two pieces. It doesn't look frayed or worn. The break in it is straight like it had been cut with scissors or a knife. No more questions. I walk out of the room and call the police.

When the officer arrives I tell him the story I'd heard and show him the strap. "This didn't tear or rip," he says. "It was deliberately cut." Later that morning he interviews the staff member. Their conclusion? New to his job, working alone while giving Matthew a shower, he leaves my son unattended on a changing table. Matthew falls off the table onto the floor. Panicked, the young man uses a pair of scissors to cut the strap and create an alibi.

Next steps happen quickly. I contact the state disability office. The employee is fired and his name is flagged to prevent him from ever again working in a care facility. All good steps, but I don't stop there. I meet with a lawyer who advises me to file suit against the group home. I'm hesitant. Why would I legally confront people still caring for my son. "Look at the bigger picture," the lawyer says. "Measures like this are sometimes needed to get everybody's attention. This will protect your son. It will also protect other people living in that facility."

We go ahead. Within days the case is settled and the group home owners agree to inspect the lifts and safety straps at all of their Twin Cities facilities. (Some equipment with lapsed expiration dates is found and replaced.) New training and inspection procedures were also implemented. All of the residents living in those homes were indeed safer.

Overall it was a terrible experience but I still feel good about the aftermath and my part in it. This time I put on my "advocate hat." I had Matthew's back, asked hard questions, and demanded accountability. It helped him, and others, too.

How do we serve our children as good advocates?

Choose the right battles. Be smart about when and where to advocate. If we're constantly confronting doctors, nurses, therapists, and teachers, they might just write us off as chronic complainers or over-meddling parents. Don't back down, but don't create confrontation at every turn, either.

Be respectful. For the most part we're dealing with well-trained, well-meaning, competent professionals. Respect them and their skills.

Similar respect needs to be returned to us. We need to work together to solve problems and help our children, not to win advocacy points.

Do your homework. Caring for children with disabilities creates complex and complicated situations. Learn what you need to know. We aren't doctors, but we can read and ask questions. The internet can (usually) be a great resource, along with books and articles. Other parents, too. When tough situations or conflicts arise, be a credible, informed participant.

Be creative. In the mid-1950s John Holter's son was born with spina bifida and developed life-threatening hydrocephalus ("water on the brain"). A toolmaker by trade, Holter went to his basement workshop and developed a prototype for a small pump (or shunt) that has since helped millions of similarly-affected children (including my own son). Who knows the impact your creative skills might have?

Avoid useless anger. When "fighting" for your child, anger can sometimes be justified and might even empower advocacy in positive ways. But don't let emotions get out of control or let the situation become about you. Advocacy should always be about what's best for your child.

Find good allies. In times of conflict, it helps to bring in other people for objectivity and expertise. I attended many school IEP meetings for my sons. I was impressed by one school district that assigned a "designated advocate" to attend those meetings whose only job was to make sure student needs remained top priority. A great and helpful idea!

Advocating for your child will have challenges, but don't back down. Put on that hat! You'll stand a little taller and feel a little prouder. More important, your child's needs will be better met. That's what advocacy is all about.

Smiles

Humor is healing. The smiles and laughter that come into your child's life are priceless gifts. Welcome the wonderful people who bring them! Our kids need to smile. So do we. Make sure to create and enjoy some of your own.

Dads like us live in a pretty serious world most of the time, with most days bringing at least some levels of stress and worry. That can wear us down. To balance that out we need humor and more than a few smiles. Laughter helps relieve stress, lifts depression and calms anxiety. Like exercise, it is free medicine that should be prescribed and taken daily.

Years ago the writer Norman Cousins, hospitalized with severe pain due to arthritis and heart disease, was frustrated when meds brought him no relief. He checked himself out of the hospital and into a hotel where over the course of several days he binge-watched his favorite comedy movies. "Ten minutes of hearty laughter gave me two hours of pain-free sleep," Cousins later wrote. "I called it belly laugh therapy." He recovered, went on to write more best-selling books (including one about the healing power of humor), and lived ten years longer than his doctor predicted.

Actor-comedian Bill Murray describes a similar experience. "I wasn't clinically depressed," he says, "but I was definitely a bummer to be around. A friend suggested I listen to music that made me laugh. It worked. Humor helped heal me."

In our often-heavy lives, we need the lightness of laughter. The best kind sneaks up on us, especially when it comes from our kids. Both my sons enjoy humor. Matthew can laugh so hard tears squeeze from the corners of his eyes and roll down his cheeks. He also has a gift for making other people laugh at some pretty strange times. All the funnier.

One evening we invited my new boss, Rick, and his wife, Diane, over for dinner. Rick, principal at a Christian school, initially appeared quite conservative and reserved. As our guests settled into the living room, Matthew, then about eight, confidently rolled his wheelchair right up to them, flashed a big smile, and said, clear as day, "Let's talk sex!" I have no idea where that came from. I was shocked and quickly looked for their response. Rick laughed. Diane laughed. Matthew laughed. We all laughed. That ice-breaking moment jump-started a delightful friendship. Oh, Matthew!

Christmas mornings were always fun—and funny. While Matthew enthusiastically tore the wrapping paper off his presents he treated us to a running commentary on what he thought might be in each one. "I hope this isn't a bowling ball," was a favorite line. So was, "I think this is cigarettes!" No bowling balls or cigarettes, but lots of laughter. Thank you, Matthew!

He could be a stinker, too, but even that brought smiles. He went through a phase—I'm still not sure why—when the words "I hate you!" frequently came out of his mouth. Too frequently. He was saying it pretty much daily to me, his mom, his nurses, everybody. We repeatedly told him not to say it. Christina, his favorite nurse, a kind and gentle young lady, after hearing it for the umpteenth time one day confronted him firmly: "Matthew, we don't want to hear that anymore! It's not nice to hate!" He knew he was being scolded. He paused, then looked at her with a shy, heart-melting smile. "Okay," he said. "I hate you, Pumpkin!"

Andrew has a way with a funny line, too. "How are you today, buddy?" I'll ask. "I'm perpendicular!" he'll answer. One evening a high fever left him unconscious and we called 911. By the time the ambulance arrived, he started to come around. An EMT still asked him the standard questions that gauge awareness. "Who's the President of the United States?" she asked. Andrew's answer? "He's the person we elect every four years to run the country." We all smiled. Well, he was right.

Humor and emergencies create a strange mix. Maybe it's another way our brains protect us during extreme stress. One day in the hospital after Matthew finished his lunch of yogurt and mashed vegetables, we could tell he was in pain. Within the hour they rushed him into emergency surgery for what turned out to be a ruptured stomach. The surgeon briefed me afterwards: "There were peas everywhere!" he told me. We both started to laugh. Why? Relieved stress, I guess. I know it felt good.

If you're lucky, others will deliver the gift of smiles into your child's life. Don't take them for granted. Most people are cautious, tentative, even uncomfortable around kids with special needs. They usually back off and I understand that. When you meet people confident enough to be funny with your kid, go for it.

Nurse Mary could tease and tickle Matthew until his face exploded with laughter. Dick E., a dear man struggling with his own paralyzing muscular disease, would lay aside his own crutches to sit on the ground for face-to-face smiles with my son. Andrew loved to bowl. He chose to do it by crawling out to the foul line and pushing the ball towards the pins. Jonathan, his able-bodied friend (and later a Marine Corps drill sergeant), watched that with a big smile, then crawled out to bowl the same way—to everyone's delight. Grampa Bob was a serious and successful businessman whose greatest joy was making his grandkids smile. He wasn't above wearing a blue fright wig to make that happen.

Dad, you need to laugh, too. Find the things that spark smiles in your life—certain friends, movies, books, TV shows, songs, favorite comedians, whatever. "Everybody needs brain candy once in a while," a counselor once told me. Don't forget to take your own humor "medicine!"

Create smiles for your kids, too. Dads can get bogged down dwelling on disabilities and special needs. Make sure you add laughter to your kid's daily "med chart." Do your own tickling and wrestling with them. Watch funny movies and TV shows together, especially in hospital rooms, when that works. Try a little carpool karaoke. They need that. You need that.

Dad, don't forget the smiles.

18

Crisis Points

Crises happen. They arrive unexpectedly in frightening, jarring moments of illness, injury or accident. Nothing totally prepares or protects us from the shock when they hit. Being realistic and learning to look at the big picture does help.

Being a dad like us is no day at the beach. Wait a minute. That's exactly what it is.

Picture yourself standing at the ocean where surf and sand meet. You look towards the horizon and see waves forming. Those waves build and move towards shore—and towards you. Most are small, and by the time they reach you they harmlessly lap at your toes and then totally disappear.

Then there are the big waves. They get your attention! You see them coming towards you, picking up speed, rising, swirling, pounding, then breaking. If you aren't standing firm when they crash over you big waves can knock you off your feet. But, very quickly, they're gone, too. The surf calms down. Everything is quiet and peaceful again. Then, out towards the horizon, new waves are forming. They're headed your way. That's how it goes at the beach.

That's how it goes for dads like us, too. Waves—let's call them crisis points—come at us. Most are small, a few are bigger, a handful are downright scary. Some are big and strong enough to knock us off our feet.

What do our waves look like with our kids? They come in all shapes and sizes. A wave might be a sudden illness, a fall that becomes an ER visit, or an unexpected surgery. One night a frantic staff member called from the group home because my son had accidentally received a potentially lethal double-dose of medicine. An EMT was on-the-scene administering Narcan and, thankfully, it worked. That was definitely a big wave, but it passed quickly.

Waves aren't always a medical crisis. They might be a school-related blow-up, a classroom meltdown, a conflict with a bully. Maybe your next crisis won't have anything to do with your child who is disabled. One of your other kids gets sick. Your teen has a car accident. Your wife receives unsettling medical news. Maybe a storm blows a chunk of roof off your house. We never know what wave will hit next. Or how big it will be.

Is there anything we can do to prepare ourselves for a crisis before it hits? How do we stay on our feet when they do? Consider these three strategies.

First, expect waves. A little boy standing at the beach says, "Look, Mommy, it just keeps flushing and flushing!" Yes, life keeps flushing. Waves keep coming. Especially for dads like us. Having realistic expectations is our best starting point.

I got knocked over by a wave recently. I called Andrew's group home to check on his day. "He isn't here," the staff person said shakily. "He just left in an ambulance." I jumped into my car for a two-hour, white-knuckle race to the hospital. By the time I arrived visiting hours had ended. It all felt like a big wave and it certainly knocked me over. After an embarrassing flash of temper, my wife wisely helped me calm down and we talked our way in. I got to Andrew, connected with his doctor who diagnosed a serious but treatable blood clot, and within days my son was headed home. A big wave had come—and passed.

It's hard to hear, but true. Expect waves. Standing with our back to the ocean is no way to live. Pretending there won't be any waves doesn't keep them away. It certainly doesn't help us keep standing when they do crash. We shouldn't live in fear of them, but know that they're out there.

Second, enjoy the lulls. Life keeps flushing and waves keep coming. Thankfully there are also quiet spaces between waves called lulls. You don't know when your lulls will come or how long they'll last, so when they do, float in the calm and enjoy them fully. You've earned that.

Third, see the whole beach. A beach is more than ocean. It is more than waves. It is bright sunshine, cool breezes, seagulls soaring high overhead, puffy white clouds, kids building sand castles, happy people relaxing and playing together. There's so much to see and enjoy at the beach. If you remember to look.

Sometimes we get so wrapped up with our "waves" that we forget to look at the whole beach. Big crises demand our full attention, for sure. But we shouldn't get so consumed by them (or fearful of them) that we fail to see everything else. Taking care of our kids is a priority. But life is more than that.

You and I have children who are disabled. We also have marriages, family relationships, friendships, jobs, creative pursuits, hobbies, and things we just like to do. There's a lot of good stuff on our beach! YOLO (you only live once) is as true for us as it is for everyone else. When waves crash in and knock us over—and they will—let's get back up, shake the water out of our ears, take a deep breath, and move on.

Sound simple? It's actually one of the hardest things dads must do. But we have to! For everyone's sake, let's make the most of our days at the beach.

19
Pride

You can and should feel great pride in your child. Our pride might look a bit different from what other dads experience, but it's just as real. It might even run a little deeper. Don't forget to save a little for yourself, too.

Dads love bragging about their kids. You see it on their bumper stickers. You read it in their Facebook posts. Mostly you see it when their eyes light up as they describe the goal their son scored in last night's hockey game or when they tell you their daughter is headed off to a great college next fall. Dads are proud of their kids and want others to know it.

Good for them! Why shouldn't dads feel proud? Bragging about our kids is a natural instinct that feels great. You may not hear these exact words, but a proud dad's message is loud and clear: "Hey, look at my kid!"

Dads like us feel proud, too. But let's be honest—it is different. Our pride won't be prompted by academic honor lists, football heroics, or musical skills. But our pride is still there. Quieter, perhaps, but feelings of delight and joy that are just as real as anyone else's. "Hey, look at my kid, too!"

Andrew loves sports, both watching and playing. A great "proud papa" moment for me was cheering him on as he completed a 1-mile run in elementary school, on crutches no less. (Later he finished a number of 5K wheelchair races). In both junior and senior high he played adaptive sports: wheelchair basketball, soccer, floor hockey, softball, and bowling. He even tried his hand at adapted golf. Those activities were the highlight of his school years. Mine, too. It meant lots of carpools and bleacher-butt but I wouldn't trade those memories for anything.

Watching Andrew and his teammates was more than fun. To see those young boys and girls, disabled, physically and mentally challenged, a few missing arms and legs, battling muscles with minds of their own, was inspiring. It also gave me a new perspective on true athletic performance.

Picture two basketball players lined up to shoot a free throw. Both are 15 feet away from a basket 10 feet off the ground. The first athlete is LeBron James, 6' 9", 250 pounds of toned muscle, built like a locomotive. After decades of daily practice, LeBron shoots with ease and makes about 8 out of every 10 free throws. LeBron shoots, he usually scores. Impressive.

Our second athlete is Bobby, age 11. I watched him play wheelchair basketball many times and shoot many free throws. Bobby doesn't stand at the free throw line, he sits in his chair, about 3 ½ feet tall. The referee hands him the ball. Bobby uses his left hand to push back a few feet, then propels forward with the ball in his right hand. As he comes to the line he flings the ball toward the basket in a high arc. If he's lucky, the ball might hit the front rim. Usually he misses. When the ball caroms off the backboard and falls through the net (one out of 50 times, if that), you can't believe the cheers that erupt in the gymnasium! Hats off to LeBron, but a whole bigger level of impressive, if you ask me.

Think about Bobby for a second living his life from a wheelchair. You might expect to find him mostly at home, watching TV, maybe playing video games. Not Bobby, and not many boys and girls like him. They get out there to play and do their (adapted) best. Sitting somewhere in the stands at that game is Bobby's dad, no doubt bursting with pride. He should be!

This goes beyond sports. Maybe for your child it's music, painting, being in a play, doing some kind of craft work. Maybe they like to read or enjoy video games. They adapt their skills to activities they enjoy. That surprises us and fills us with pride, too, just like other dads. (If you have a minute I'd like to tell you about the time Andrew made a free throw!) Go ahead and say it—hey, look at my kid!

There's an even deeper level of pride for dads like us. I'm writing this in the spring of 2020. My son, Matthew, now 39, lives in a group home in Maple Grove, Minnesota, receiving medical care 24/7. He spends 100% of his time in a hospital bed or large recliner, dozing in and out of consciousness. When prompted he can move his hands, but just barely. When awake he looks around, smiles at me and his nurses, listens to music and loves having books read to him. A very quiet, inactive life, as most people would see it.

How do I see it? Am I proud of Matthew? You betcha! Why? It's a pride based not on my son's "doing" but in his "being." Matthew's doctor recently described him this way. "This young man can't do many things, but he does one thing remarkably well—he stays alive!" My son has battled overcome dozens of life-threatening illnesses, surgeries, and health crises. His will to live, his perseverance, his stamina, his ability to bounce back, has amazed and delighted all of us for decades. Most impressive, Matthew has done all that with a calm, sweet, peaceful spirit. Hey, look at my kid!

Dad, are you feeling proud about your son or daughter? I hope so. How do we best do that?

Put on "new glasses." See your child's special attributes. Rise above our culture's superficial worship of physical looks and athletic achievements. So many things in life are more valuable and longer-lasting than that. The world our kids live in—and the world we're privileged to share with them—shows us life in new and amazing ways.

Avoid jealousy. It's easy to feel jealous about experiences other dads get to share with their kids. It must be quite a kick to see your kid star in a high school basketball game or get a college scholarship. Applaud those achievements. But beware of letting jealousy sink into bitterness. Don't go there! Celebrate what your child can do, encourage them, enjoy it with them. That's good for them and for you.

Help your child find activities they excel in and enjoy. Maybe for them it will be adapted sports. Maybe it's in the arts. Many folks who are disabled love to fish. A local theater company, comprised totally of young actors who are all developmentally disabled, produces fun shows and changes lives. Our digital, high-tech world is opening doors unheard of a decade ago. Help your child find those doors. Search the web, make phone calls, talk to other parents. Teachers and case managers can help. Find places where your kid can shine!

Feel proud of your child, and feel proud of yourself, too. That may sound self-focused but let's just say it. Being a dad like us isn't easy. No one knows what your parenting experience is really like except you. You're doing your best. You aren't perfect. You get worn down and make mistakes. We all have moments we'd like to do over. But you're hanging in there—physically, mentally, emotionally. You'll probably never say this out loud, but give yourself permission to at least feel it. "Hey, look at me!" Pass a little pride around. Go ahead, dad, you deserve it!

20

Gratitude

Make the wise choice to be thankful every day.

Dads do lots of hard stuff. We wait nervously while our child is in surgery. We sit through long, sometimes draining meetings with teachers and social workers. We juggle daily demands of marriage, job, parenting, and more. This might be the most difficult of all—doing all that while trying to be grateful.

Gratitude is easy when kids are healthy, bills are paid, and work is going well. What happens when none of that is true? The world our kids live in, the one we share with them, is demanding. Daily caregiving pressures, nagging worries, and unexpected challenges often leave us tired, if not numb. Being thankful in those places is a real test of spirit, one we often lose.

There are deeper conflicts, too. How *can* a dad be thankful when his newborn son has Down Syndrome? When he knows that his daughter with cerebral palsy won't ever walk normally, much less down a church aisle at her wedding. How can he be thankful knowing his autistic son has a slim chance of graduating from high school and faces a lifetime of limited job opportunities? How can a dad be grateful when his child's untreatable medical diagnosis threatens to shorten his life?

Gratitude can be hard. Bitter comes easy. So does self-pity. Years ago I knew a father whose teenage daughter, the shining light of his life, died tragically. His grief and anger hardened into bitterness, leaving him emotionally paralyzed. His last years were spent alone in a dark room watching TV and drinking beer. One tragedy became two. That won't happen to us, we think. But living with an ungrateful spirit can drain the joy from our lives in a thousand little ways.

Gratitude is more than a feeling. It's a deliberate choice we need to make, many times a day. Think of it as an emotional muscle requiring regular exercise. The more you "flex" it, the stronger it becomes. That happens the more we choose to be thankful for everything else in our life, including all we face with our child who is disabled.

James Autry is an author, a poet, a respected business leader, and a dad like us who has raised a child with autism. In his book *Choosing Gratitude—Learning to Love the Life You Have*, Autry says he takes a "gratitude walk" every morning. "(On that walk) I remind myself that there will always be more reasons for gratitude than despair," he says. Maybe a regular walk like that can work for you. Perhaps you write in a journal. Maybe you find five minutes each day to just sit quietly and focus on the positives. Whatever works for you, find time to flex your gratitude muscle.

What are we grateful for? First and always, for our child and the person he or she is. We're thankful for the gift of their life. Am I grateful for what my sons face being disabled? Honestly, no. I know it's a major part of who they are. It is also a big part of who I am as their dad. Learning to accept those realities and challenges isn't easy. But I am always thankful for who they are and that I am blessed to be their dad.

We're thankful, too, for key people in their lives: their moms, extended family members, friends and loved ones, their whole "parade." We're grateful, too, for all the rich, life-building adventures our children have, and for the ones we share with them.

We can be thankful for people who make special efforts to support our kids. One morning a UPS truck pulled up to our rural Minnesota home and delivered three big boxes addressed to Matthew Harris. We hadn't ordered anything so we were puzzled. In the boxes was a new Apple computer, monitor, and printer. No card was enclosed but we did find a small, almost hidden address label: "Steve Wozniak, Los Gatos, California." (You'll remember him as Steve Jobs' high school friend and the co-inventor of Apple computers). I didn't know Mr. Wozniak, but a mutual friend who did told him about my son and his love for computers. Wow. I quickly sent off a thank you letter and still enjoy that surprise to this day. Enjoy gifts in your child's life. Be thankful for them.

Fun memories trigger gratitude. I have many. Walking (and rolling) across the Golden Gate Bridge with Andrew. Taking Matthew on a beach-wheelchair ride on the sands of Monterey Bay. Holding the hands of both my boys and looking up in awe at Yosemite's Half-Dome. Using an adapted golf cart to play one hole of golf with Andrew. Taking him (and a pair of ear plugs) to a Metallica concert in Minneapolis. Watching both sons participate in high school graduation ceremonies. Re-living those moments helps me flex my gratitude muscle. What memories do that for you?

The attitude of gratitude is contagious so hang out with grateful people. My elderly friend has a standard, one-word reply whenever anyone asks her, "how are you?" It is, always, "grateful." She must have days when she's not feeling that, but grateful remains her choice. Stick close to people like that!

That describes both my sons. Andrew wrote this in a middle school essay: "I have cerebral palsy. I'm thankful I do. If I didn't, I just wouldn't be me. And I wouldn't be able to play wheelchair basketball!" A few students were invited to speak at Matthew's 6th grade graduation ceremony. When I learned my son was one of them I got very nervous. (The "Smile" chapter in this book will explain why!) I watched my little guy wheel himself up to the podium, look out at everybody, lean into the microphone, and smile. Then he said just two words: "Thank you!" Those two words were enough. They are always enough.

In the words of Melody Beattie, "Gratitude turns what we have into enough—and more." Dad, making a choice to be grateful—every day—has the power to transform your life. It will be one of the smartest things you ever do.

Be There

Your child needs you like they need no one else. Be there.

This is the shortest chapter in this book. It should be. Its message is simple. None are more important.

Dad, be there.

A child needs a dad. We know that by instinct. Studies also prove it. Children with active fathers in their lives do better. They are happier and better adjusted. They get better grades in school. They have healthier relationships. They go on to perform at a higher level in jobs, careers, all of life. They call this the "Father Effect." As someone has said, there's a dad-shaped hole in every kid's heart. There are exceptions, of course, but in the great majority of cases, it just works that way. Dads make a difference.

Why should that be any different for a child who is disabled and has special needs? You can make the case that his or her need for a dad is even greater. Our kids face bigger challenges than "normal" kids. Physically, mentally, emotionally. Bigger challenges in relationships. They are more vulnerable to bullying. A recent study says children with disabilities are twice as likely to face neglect and/or sexual, physical or mental abuse than children with no disabilities. They have a harder time fitting in than their peers. They begin life far behind in so many basic areas and spend their whole lives trying to catch up. They need all the help they can get. They need a dad.

Sadly, many children today are growing up without dads. In 1960 10 percent of kids were being raised without a father in their home. Today it is 40 percent. That's also true for kids who are disabled. Many live with single moms with no dad in the picture.

There are many reasons for that, complicated reasons. You may be a father removed from your family through separation or divorce. Dads in those situations can still be close to their kids. It will take extra work and planning but you can make that happen. You can be there.

Being there is more than physical presence, of course. It is active engagement with your child. Know him or her. Let your child know you. Share your life. Explore theirs. Talk to them. Play with them. Teach them. Discipline them. Spend time with them. Know their favorite music, ice cream, colors, and friends. Visit their classrooms. Read to them. Be at their doctor appointments, games and school events. Know what they think. Know their dreams. Know what makes them laugh—and cry. Be a hugger, a get-down-on-the-floor tickler. Be present with them. Be there.

Your little boy or girl is going to need lots of people to make it in their world. They need a loving mom, other family members, good doctors, caring nurses, trained teachers, smart therapists, positive caregivers, and so many others—the whole parade.

As much as anyone, they need *you*. They need a father who will love, care and treasure them, a dad who will be there for their first steps, and all the ones to follow.

Dad, be there.

Letting Go

Saying goodbye to your child, whenever it happens, under whatever circumstances, is painful beyond words. Starting to let go early in small ways helps. But know that all you share together never really ends.

A young parent puts their child on his or her first school bus. A middle-age parent helps their child pack for college. Older parents wave goodbye to their child after a wedding. Bittersweet farewells are a natural part of life. That doesn't make them any easier.

Goodbyes are especially hard for a dad with a son or daughter who is disabled and has special needs. You've been your child's father, provider, and protector since day one. You may have experienced that delivery room moment or been there when disability was confirmed for them. You saw their first steps or maybe their first wheelchair roll. You can't imagine not being with them, and them with you. You treasure every day you've had together and don't want those days to ever end. But transitions happen and goodbyes are waiting out there for all of us.

They can be frightening. Every parent has sleepless nights worrying about their kid's safety and wondering how they'll make it on their own. Anxieties multiply for dads like us. Our vulnerable kids, with physical and mental deficits, head into a world that can be harsh, if not brutal. Why wouldn't dads like us worry and feel protective? Next to discovering their disability, letting go has got to be the toughest moment we face.

I've experienced two major transition-points with my sons. Into his late teens, even with all his daily cares (and a bedroom that looked like a mini-ICU), Matthew always lived at home. We never considered alternatives. Somehow with the support we provided—especially the remarkable, tireless efforts of his mom—and his "parade," it all seemed to work.

Until it didn't. Matthew's 18th year was a rough one for him, and for his parents. After yet another hospitalization for pneumonia stretched into weeks, his doctor recommended Matthew be given a permanent breathing tube, or tracheotomy. That had medical benefits but also added more daily cares to his already jam-packed schedule. Andrew's complex needs were also expanding. It was time to face new realities. Something had to give.

We asked Matthew's case manager to start looking for a suitable group home and she soon located one. Only ten miles from our house, it felt like a hundred. I sat with him at the hospital after his trach surgery, waiting for medical transport. Matthew was going home. For the first time ever, it wouldn't be our home.

We had cared for our boy every day of his life. Now we were handing him over to people we didn't know to go to a place we didn't know. (One nurse gave me an odd look when I asked if I could bring my sleeping bag to occasionally stay overnight. That was strange, and I never did). We were soon taking Matthew for daily wheelchair strolls in his new neighborhood. That helped, but they were "visits." Letting go was still very hard. As I write this more than four decades later, I can still feel the sharp pain of those first days.

A second transition took place eleven years later with Andrew. Major life-changes were underway all around. Matthew was now in his third group home. Andrew was living with me and my new wife, Sue, and attending a post-high school transition program. His dream, he told me any chance he got, was to live in his own apartment. Alone. Independent. "By myself, dad."

Was that possible? I was skeptical. Could Andrew manage daily chores like cooking, laundry, and shopping? His case manager, Independent Living Skills counsellor, and others who knew him well, were all optimistic. "With support services this can work" was the consensus. A vacancy in an accessible apartment soon opened. Wow, this is great! Andrew said. Wow, this is great, I said...kind of.

My 21-year-old son was ready to go. Was I ready to let go of him? I didn't want to say goodbye. I would miss him. Never again would I be able to casually walk into his room for a spontaneous chat. Everyone promised support services would fill in any gaps, but I was still worried.

After many meetings and planning sessions, we made the decision to go for it. Gulp.

I'll never forget Andrew's "moving day." After hours of unloading furniture and boxes—and a pizza dinner to celebrate—it was time to say goodbye. I hugged him and told him I loved him and was proud of him. I started to cry. He sat quietly in his wheelchair, stoically staring at me. "You know, Dad," he said in his best reassuring voice, "it's good to be able to express your emotions." Yes, Andrew, it is. See you later.

How do dads "let go" of their child who is disabled? Remember these points:

Goodbyes are part of life—for everybody. Nothing is permanent, change happens, life moves on. You wouldn't expect or want it to be any other way.

Know you will get through it. You have already made it through difficult moments and days. You will get through your goodbyes, too.

The pain of letting go lessens with time. It never fully disappears, and that's okay. Would you really want it to?

Let go early and often. From early on our child's life becomes a series of transitions. They're born, leave the hospital, come home. In what seems like ten minutes they head to daycare, pre-school, then elementary, junior high and high school. Transitions are painful, but they happen.

A good way to ease our pain is by taking small "letting go" steps along the way. Here are some practical ways to do that:

- Plan brief but regular times away from your child, even when he or she is small.

- Explore respite care options. (Research programs for which you may qualify).

- Get comfortable leaving your child with grandparents, relatives, and trusted friends.

- Seek out good babysitters. One caution: be sensitive to other people's comfort levels when asking them to handle special-needs cares your child may require.

- Plan weekly date nights and occasional overnights with your spouse or partner.

- As your child gets older, take advantage of day care, school activities, and specialized transition programs.

- A week at an adapted summer camp is a great option.

Early, well-planned, and positive separations are good for parent and child, and teach us how to say goodbye.

Build trust in caregivers. It is very hard to trust someone else to do what you've been doing for your child. It's especially hard when that somebody else is a stranger. Don't let them stay strangers. Get to know your child's caregivers.

Tech to connect. Our digital age provides great options for staying in regular touch with loved ones even at a distance. Andrew and I email and text regularly. Facetime helps me see both my sons. Is it as good as in-person visits? No. But it helps.

Remember—we never really say goodbye. We'll have moments, days and seasons when we deeply miss our kids. Elizabeth Stone wisely said that"...being a parent is like having your heart go walking outside your body." We know what that feels like. Don't let it throw you if a few unexpected tears flow. Years ago I made a good decision to not be embarrassed when expressing those feelings. Take that, Andrew.

Letting go of our children is always painful. We get through it best by knowing our children never really leave us in thought or spirit. Never.

The Biggest Question

*Dads like us face many questions, including the
biggest one of all.*

You might read this chapter. You might not. Either way, I know I
have to write it. I do hope you read it.

It would be easier to skip what we'll talk about here. Let's call them
the big questions. Everybody asks them, but being the parent of a child
who is disabled makes them virtually unavoidable. These questions can
be painful. We struggle to answer them. Even if we never voice them out
loud, they don't go away.

We might also call these the "why" questions. Why are children born
with disabilities? More personal: why is *my* child disabled? Why does
my child have special needs? Why did this happen to *my* family? Why
did this happen to *me*?

We can't begin to address those questions in a few pages in this book.
What we can do is acknowledge them and honestly admit we wrestle
with them. That's a place to start.

This is deep, personal stuff. The "why questions" are really the God
questions. Maybe you believe in God. Maybe you don't. Either way, the
questions linger.

Here's the biggest one of all: "Where is God in all of this?" If you do
believe in God, I'm certain you've asked that big question. I have, many
times, in many ways, over many years.

I do believe in God. I read the Bible. I pray. (I don't hear God talking
to me, though, over-spiritualize things, or look for angels hovering over
hospital beds). But something did happen to me years ago in the space
of about five minutes that I've never forgotten. Those moments changed
the way I face my "why" questions. This is the story of Matthew's Star.

* * * * * *

On a cold, blustery winter morning in January, 1981, a little before 7 a.m., I drive to the University of Massachusetts Medical Center before work to visit my son, Matthew. I know this hospital well. My son has spent the first three months of his life here. Doctors are doing all they can but honestly tell us they aren't sure he's going to make it.

I trudge across the icy parking lot feeling tired. Exhausted, really. I'm also feeling angry. The big questions are slamming me. God, where are You? Do You care about Matthew? Do You care about what's happening here? Do you care about me? God, where is all his headed? The questions might be prayers but they're spoken through clenched teeth.

Here's where my story gets a little "out there." I remember walking away from my car that morning feeling tired and angry at God. Less than five minutes later I reach the hospital lobby and those feelings have dramatically changed. Suddenly I feel energized. My anger is gone, replaced by a peaceful calm. The change is so abrupt I sit in the hospital lobby to process what just happened.

An image forms in my mind. It is a gold star with five points. Each point has a one-sentence phrase next to it. This sounds strange, I know. I can't explain it. All I know is that when I got out of my car that morning I did not have that picture in my head. When I reached the lobby, I did. I can still see that star clearly and each of its five messages. This is what they said.

"I am in control."

Since the day Matthew was born life has felt out of control, a chaotic, exhausting, jumbled mess, lurching from one crisis to the next. God is saying to me, I am in control. This is not meaningless chaos. Everything going on is in My hands. My perfect plan is being worked out. You may not see or understand it all right now, but know that I am in control. Trust Me, God says.

"I love Matthew—even more than you do."

Knowing God is in control makes life feel secure. But Matthew's physical suffering is so hard on him. God, if You are in control, why are

You allowing this to happen? Don't You love Matthew? God says, I do love Matthew. I love him even more than you do. Remember, I created Him. His life is in My hands. They are hands of love. You may not always see or feel that, but it is true. Trust Me, God says.

"I love you, too."

Matthew's suffering has been hard on him. It has been hard on everyone who loves him. As his dad, watching all this has been horrible. Some days it feels like punishment. I question whether or not God loves me. God says, I do love you. This is not punishment. I have not abandoned you. I am here with you in every moment. Trust Me, God says.

"I will make all things beautiful in My time."

Dark thoughts weigh me down. I know my son will not lead a normal life. I'm not even sure he'll be alive much longer. I need that darkness lifted. I need hope. I need to know there will be a time of no more spina bifida, no more disabilities, no more surgeries, no more hospitals, no more pain, no more tears. God says, I promise you that hope. I will make all things beautiful in My time. Trust Me, God says.

"Until then, I'll give you strength. One day at a time."

Hope for a perfect "someday" is wonderful. But how do I make it through today? I want to be strong. So often I feel weak. God says, find the strength you need in Me. I will be here with you. I will give you all you need, one day at a time. Sometimes one hour at a time, even one moment at a time. Trust Me, God says.

* * * * * * * *

The five messages of Matthew's Star came to me unexpectedly that winter morning more than forty years ago and turned that day around. That's not to say all difficult moments or struggles ended at that point.

Far from it. Life presented more crises for Matthew, for all of us, in coming months and years. Andrew's physical and mental decline—not "typical" for cerebral palsy, doctors told me—was slow but undeniable. Pam began exhibiting Parkinson's-like symptoms in her late 40s and passed away in 2012. Genetic testing surprisingly revealed all three shared a rare and incurable neurological disorder called Pelizaeus-Merzbacher Disease (PMD). There would be more cold winter mornings.

Challenges remain. What also remains—stronger and brighter than ever—is Matthew's Star. Those five messages are as real and powerful to me now as they have ever been. Through it all, they are enough. Because He is enough.

We each walk our own personal path. Mine includes the gift of Matthew's Star. Thank you for letting me share it with you.

* * * * * * * * * * * *

I began writing this chapter in the early morning hours of October 5, 2020. A little before noon that day I received a phone call from North Memorial Hospital in Minneapolis. Matthew had just been brought to their ER running a high fever. The diagnosis came quickly—he had sepsis, a serious, life-threatening blood infection. Four days later, four days shy of his 40th birthday, Matthew Richard Harris took his last earthly breath. On his grave marker, below his name and the dates of his life, is a star. A simple, five-pointed star.

Thank You, Dad

There are three little words dads like us probably don't hear very often. "Thank you, Dad."

Why we want to hear them, why we like to hear them, or whether we should need to hear them, are all good questions. Let's leave them for another time. For now, let's just honestly admit it: hearing "thank you, Dad" makes us feel good.

Why don't we hear it more often? Different reasons. Our kids may not fully grasp what we do for them. They may take it for granted, not in a bad way, but because they correctly sense this is what fathers naturally do for their children. Maybe they don't say it because of physical or mental limitations. Matthew lost the ability to speak in the final years of his life. Perhaps your son or daughter isn't able to express those words—or any words—to you.

When we do hear "thank you," it does feel good. It touches us deeply. It affirms the value of all we do for our kids. Hearing those words or not, we'll keep loving and caring for them. That's a given. But I want to close this book by saying it anyway.

Thank you, Dad. I hope you hear that. I hope you feel it.

Thank you for all you have done for your child who has disabilities and special needs. Our situations, families, and caregiving are all unique. Only you know what you've done and are doing. For all of it, thank you, Dad.

Thank you for hanging in there for your kids. We get tired and frustrated sometimes. More often than we admit we reach what we think is the end of our rope. You have held on! You are holding on! You continue to "be there."

Thank you for all you have done and are doing for your wife or partner. (A special word of thanks to them, as well!) Thanks, too, dad, for all you've done for your other children and family members. Only you know what that really looks like.

Thank you for reading this book. It may seem a small thing, but it means you've given valuable time to confront hard stuff concerning yourself and your child. That says something good and positive about you.

We share a difficult journey. But we keep moving ahead. May you find the strength, courage, and wisdom you will need for every step to come.

Thank you, Dad. May God bless you and your precious child.

A TOOL KIT

- Learning the Language
- To Think About
- Planning for the Future
- Support Organizations: Contact Info
- More Reading

Learning the Language

When you become the father of a child who is disabled you enter a world with a language all its own. From early on you'll hear words, phrases and acronyms from doctors, nurses, therapists, teachers, and others that you've probably never heard before.

This is frustrating! These people are talking about your child. You want and need to understand what they're saying. Here are some words (and brief definitions) for starters. Your child's situation and diagnosis is unique—feel free to add a few of your own!

-A-

ADHD...Attention Deficit Hyperactivity Disorder.

AFO...Ankle Foot Orthosis...a brace/device that aids walking by supporting lower-leg muscles.

-B-

Barium...a chalky liquid used in testing procedures such as a barium swallow test.

-C-

Cleft Palate...a congenital opening in the upper lip or roof of the mouth that may extend into the nose.

CPR...Cardio Pulmonary Resuscitation.

CSF...Cerebrospinal Fluid...the colorless bodily fluid that surrounds the brain and spinal cord.

CT Scan...Computerized Tomography Scan creates a cross-sectional image of the soft tissues in the body.

-D-

DHS...Department of Human Services.

DNR...Do Not Resuscitate...an order directing that a patient should not receive CPR if his or her heart stops.

-E-

EBD...Emotional Behavior Disorder.

EEG...Electroencephalography...records the electrical activity of the brain.

EKG...Electrocardiography...records the electrical activity of the heart.

EMG...Electromyography...records the electrical activity of skeletal muscles.

Epilepsy...a group of neurological disorders resulting in recurrent seizures.

-F-

FMLA...Family Medical Leave Act...legislation that protects the work status of employees facing long-term medical needs within his or her family.

Foley Catheter...a flexible tube that passes into the bladder to drain urine.

-G-

Gastrostomy (or G) Tube...an external tube placed directly into the stomach to provide nutrition, liquids, and medications.

GJ Tube...an external tube placed directly into the stomach and small intestine (or jejunum) to provide nutrition, liquids, and medications.

GI-Series...x-rays of the (upper or lower) gastrointestinal tract.

Global Developmental Delay...umbrella term for a child significantly delayed in his or her physical and cognitive development.

-H-

Health Directive...defines an individual's preferences regarding medical treatments and interventions.

Hemophilia...an inherited human genetic disease that makes it difficult for the body to form blood clots, which in turn, stop bleeding.

Hospice Care...specialized nursing care focused on quality of life (and comfort care) for patients who are terminally ill.

Hospitalist...a hospital-based doctor specializing in the care of acutely-ill patients.

Hydrocephalus...a physical disorder characterized by an abnormal increase in cerebrospinal fluid in the ventricles of the brain.

-I-

IDEA...Individuals with Disabilities Education Act...the initial law (later reauthorized and updated) making free appropriate public education available to all eligible children.

IEP...Individualized Education Plan...a legal document developed for each public-school student in the U.S. who needs special education.

ILS Counselor...Independent Living Skills Counselor...a trained professional who provides support in specialized independent living skills.

Incontinence...uncontrolled leakage of urine.

Infiltrate...when a substance or cells move into areas and organs of the body.

ISP...Individual Support Plan.

IV...Intravenous Infusion...administering fluids, medication, and nutrients directly into a person's vein.

-M-

MA...Medicaid...a government program that providing health insurance for adults and children with limited income and resources.

Meningitis...an acute or chronic inflammation of the protective membranes (the meninges) that cover the brain and spinal cord.

MRSA...Methicillin-resistant Staphylococcus Aureus...an infection caused by a type of staph bacteria resistant to many antibiotics used to treat staph infections.

MRI...Magnetic Resonance Imaging...a medical imaging technique that sees inside the body to form cross-sectional images of various organs.

-N-

Nebs...treatment from a nebulizer which turns medicine into a mist.

Neurologist...a doctor specializing in the diagnosis and treatment of conditions and diseases involving the nervous system, including the brain, spinal cord and nerves

Neurosurgeon...a doctor specializing in the surgical treatment of conditions and diseases involving the nervous system, including the brain, spinal cord and nerves

NICU...Neo-Natal Intensive Care Unit...also called an intensive care nursery, the hospital unit specializing in the care of ill or premature newborn infants.

NG-Tube...Nasogastric Intubation...the insertion of a plastic tube through the nose, down the esophagus, into the stomach, for the purpose of administering medicine and nutrition.

NPO..."Nothing by Mouth"...the period of time before a surgery or procedures when the patient cannot have anything to eat or drink.

Nurse Practitioner...an advanced practice registered nurse.

-O-

OT...Occupational Therapy...uses assessment and intervention to develop, recover or maintain the common activities (or occupations) of a patient.

-P-

PA...Physician Assistant or Physician Associate.

Palliative Care...healthcare that focuses on quality of life and the relieving and preventing of pain.

PCA...Personal Care Attendant.

Pedi-ICU...Pediatric Intensive Care Unit...a hospital unit specializing in the care of critically ill infants, children, teenagers, and young adults, ages 0-21.

Pedodontist...also called a pediatric dentist, specializes in the dental care of children.

Phlebotomy...the process of making a puncture in a vein for the purpose of drawing blood.

PIC Line...Peripherally-Inserted Central Catheter...an intravenous access used to administer medicines for a prolonged period of time.

Pneumonia...an infection that inflames air sacs in the lungs, causing them to fill with fluid.

PT...Physical Therapy...a type of therapy using specially-designed exercises and equipment to help a patient regain or improve his or her physical abilities.

POLST...Physicians Orders for Life-Sustaining Treatment.

Pulse Oximeter...a device that measures how much oxygen is in a patient's blood.

-R-

RSDI...Retirement, Survivors, and Disability Insurance...government benefits paid to workers, their dependents, and survivors.

Respite Care...planned or emergency temporary care provided to care-givers of a child or adult.

RSV...Respiratory Syncytial Virus...a common, contagious virus causing infections of the respiratory tract.

-S-

Seizure...commonly referred to as an epileptic seizure, a combination of symptoms caused by abnormally excessive neuronal activity in the brain.

Sepsis...a potentially life-threatening condition when an infection causes injury to the body's own tissues and organs.

Shock...a medical condition caused by insufficient blood flow to bodily tissues.

Sonogram...Ultrasound Scan...the use of high frequency sound waves to create images from inside the body.

SSA...Social Security Administration.

SSI...Supplemental Security Income...monthly financial payments provided to people with disabilities and older adults who have little or no income or resources.

Stroke...when lessened blood flow to the brain causes the death of brain cells.

-T-

TBI...Traumatic Brain Injury...injury and/or trauma to the brain caused by an external force.

-U-

Urologist...a doctor specializing in kidney and bladder function.

UTI...Urinary Tract Infection.

-W-

Waivered Services...provides funding for services in place of institutional care.

NOTES:

To Think About

We've identified many (but certainly not all) topics in this book that dads like us think about. The following question-prompts from each chapter can help you think deeper about and personally apply what you've read.

INTRODUCTION - WELCOME TO THE CLUB

- When did you first learn about your child's disability?

- How did you feel at that point?

- Who helped you the most during that time?

CHAPTER 1 - SHOCK

- Did you experience emotional shock when you learned your child was disabled?

- What helped you start to process all that was happening?
- Do you remember moments or conversations that helped you during that time?

CHAPTER 2 - SADNESS

- When did you first feel sad about your child's disability?

- How did you first express your sadness, and has that changed over time?

- What do you most celebrate about your child?

CHAPTER 3 - ANGER

- Have you felt "angry" about your child's disability?

- What does anger look like on you?

- What helps you best manage your anger?

Chapter 4 - The Parade

- How do you feel about your child's "parade?"

- How did you react the first time a key member of your child's parade left?

- What's one thing you can do—today—to help your child's parade run more smoothly?

Chapter 5 - Doctors

- Who are the key doctors overseeing your child's care?

- Have you ever felt intimidated or disrespected by a doctor? What did you do?

- How might you improve communications with your child's current medical team?

Chapter 6 - Nurses

- Who have been key nurses in your child's care?

- When was a time when a nurse provided special care for your child?

- How have you—or will you—express thanks to your child's nursing team?

CHAPTER 7 - THERAPISTS

- What therapists have made a lasting difference in your child's life?

- What are current therapy goals for your child?

- What are 2-3 things your child *can* do that makes you feel very proud of them?

CHAPTER 8 - SOCIAL WORKERS

- Who have been the most helpful social workers in your child's life?

- Have you created a plan for organizing your child's records? Is it working?

- Have you shared your hopes and dreams—and those of your child—with their social worker?

CHAPTER 9 - HOSPITALS

- What was the most difficult part about your child's most recent hospital stay?

- What helps your child, your family, and you best deal with hospital time?

- What practical suggestions would you share with your hospital staff?

CHAPTER 10 - SCHOOL

- What do you want most for your child out of their school?

- Who are 2-3 key teachers who have best helped your child?

- Is your child's current IEP "working?" How might it be improved?

CHAPTER 11 - LONELINESS

- When do you feel most "different" from other dads?

- Are you connecting with a friend (or two) on a regular basis?

- When was the last time you took a risk and went "flying?"

CHAPTER 12 - CAREER

- How is your current work-life balance?

- How are you communicating well with key people at work about your family needs?

- Do you currently have a work mentor? Is there someone who might fill that role?

CHAPTER 13 - SELF-CARE

- How is your "self-care" currently going?

- How do you fit physical exercise into your regular routine?

- When is your next scheduled "play" time?

CHAPTER 14 - MARRIAGE

- How has being the parents of a child with a disability had an impact on your marriage?

- Do you and your spouse/partner currently receive counselling support?
- When is the next scheduled "date" with your spouse/partner?

CHAPTER 15 - FAMILY TIES

- What response and feelings did family members show about your child's disability?

- How is your current communication with relatives concerning your child and family needs?

- How would you say your child's grandparents are handling all of this?

CHAPTER 16 - ADVOCATE

- Does advocating for your child come easy or difficult for you?

- When was the last time you had to advocate for your child?

- Is there a situation currently where you're hesitant to wear your "advocate hat?

CHAPTER 17 - SMILES

- What makes your child smile?

- Who are the people that make your child laugh?

- When was the last time you went with your child to his or her happy place?

CHAPTER 18 - CRISIS-POINTS

- What was the last "wave" that hit you? How did you handle it?

- How are you making the most of the "lulls" in your life?

- Are you seeing and enjoying your whole "beach"?

CHAPTER 19 - PRIDE

- What makes you most proud about your son or daughter?

- How do you share your pride with others?

- Do you feel proud about what you do as a dad like us?

CHAPTER 20 - GRATITUDE

- What are 2-3 specific things you are most thankful for about your child?

- How do you regularly "exercise" your gratitude muscle?

- Who do you know who consistently models a thankful spirit?

CHAPTER 21 - BE THERE

- What are the most difficult moments to "be" with your child? Why?

- How are you getting to really know your child?

- How are you helping your child get to know you?

CHAPTER 22 - LETTING GO

- What have been painful "letting go" moments for you to this point?

- Who are the people you most trust with your child's care?

- How are you building good relationships with your child's caregivers?

CHAPTER 23 - THE BIGGEST QUESTION

- What are the big questions you have about your child's disability?

- Have you ever talked about those questions with anyone?

- What do you do with your unanswered questions?

CHAPTER 24 - THANK YOU, DAD

- What are the ways in which you sense your child's appreciation of you?

- When was the last time you thanked your wife/partner for her role in your child's life?

- How does it feel to be thanked for being a dad like us?

Planning for the Future

Dads have a lot to think about when it comes to their child who is disabled. Medical needs, of course. Decisions about therapy, schools, special programs. Most of those worries, especially early on, are in-your-face, right now kinds of issues. You sense there are long-term things to figure out, too, like housing and employment and all that, but those can wait. Too stressful. Let's just get through today.

Planning for the future isn't something we can or should ignore for long. Even in our child's early years, there are things we need to be thinking about. With the help of good, experienced people that can happen.

What kind of planning are we talking about? Medical issues, like **health directives**. Legal matters, like **guardianships**. Financial concerns, like **special needs trusts**. The kinds of planning that address the often-scary "what-if" questions. No wonder we push estate planning to the back burner. (Most people do; the latest Gallup poll says less than half of Americans have an adequate will.) But families like ours have complicated matters to address. The sooner the better.

These issues are made more complicated because we're dealing with federal government benefit programs, state regulations that vary depending on where you live, county programs, and the like. Quite the jungle. But it's a jungle we have to figure out, especially because it includes paying for medical bills and other needed-services. Our kids have lots of those and they're very expensive. Help is out there, but we need to find out about it and how it can help our family.

I am no expert in these areas. Estate planning for my kids has not been my strength, to be honest. But here are simple words of encouragement for all of us dads, at whatever point we sit in our child's journey. In fact, just two things to do when it comes to your child's future planning.

1. START NOW.

2. GET A LAWYER.

Locate a good lawyer experienced in the area of disability law. Where do you look? Ask your child's social worker and/or case manager. Get referrals from other parents who have children with special needs.

Research the internet. Plan introductory consultations (those are usually free). There are good people out there. You'll find them. Start ASAP.

Here are a few basic terms you'll want to be familiar with as you begin your research.

GUARDIANSHIP: Depending on your child's status at age 18 it may be determined that a "guardian" (sometimes called a "conservator") is needed to oversee his or her legal and financial affairs. Guardians—appointed by the court—make the big decisions (i.e. medical decisions, where they'll live, how their money will be spent, etc.). I've been the legal guardian for both my sons. It means initiating court proceedings to get that established and completing annual forms. But it is not overly-intensive and it gives you the legal standing to be fully-involved in every facet of your child's life.

SPECIAL NEEDS AND SUPPLEMENTAL TRUSTS: Your child's financial assets need to be carefully monitored. They directly affect his or her eligibility for government benefit programs (such as SSI). A special needs/supplemental trust can be established on their behalf. All of your child's assets, such as money, bonds, insurance policies, etc. can be placed in the trust. The funds belong to the trust, not your child. The trust will need trustees, people (probably parents but others, too) who will make decisions about the resources in the trust. These resources are meant to "supplement" government benefits that come to the child. A good lawyer will help you establish the trusts and answer any questions you (or others) may have about them.

Bottom line: work with good people, get needed advice, fill out the forms, monitor changes, and communicate consistently with he people and agencies overseeing your child's case.

Long-term planning and answering difficult "what-if" questions is stressful. What's more stressful? Ignoring all this and having to do (or have others do) this thinking/planning during an emergency. Getting things in place ahead of time is much better, for us, for our child, for everyone involved.

Support Agencies: Contact Information

Autism Society
Autismsociety.org

Cleft Palate
American Cleft-Palate-Craniofacial Association
Acpacares.org

Cystic Fibrosis Foundation
cff.org

Epilepsy Foundation
epilepsy.com

Muscular Dystrophy Association
mda.org

National Down Syndrome Society
ndss.org

PACER Center
A parent training and information center for families
of children and youth with disabilities.
Pacer.org

Pelizaeus-Merzbacher Foundation
pmdfoundation.org

Spina Bifida Association
Spinabifidaassociation.org

United Cerebral Palsy
Ucp.org